NOTHING IS WASTED

A Memoir of God's Goodness in
Every Season of Life

David Rose

renownpublishing

Praise for *Nothing Is Wasted* by David Rose

David has a remarkable story that truly captures the heart of its readers in his book, *Nothing Is Wasted*. His raw, authentic, and open testimonial speaks of his perseverance and character through seasons of unimaginable heartache. His experiences could have tainted his perspective on life, but instead he chose to do something positive and created To Give A Smile, a nonprofit that has impacted children and their families around the world enduring medical hardships. His story has inspired me, and I believe will be a true encouragement to you as well.

Jill Cumnock
Chief Executive Officer, Ronald McDonald House of Dallas

From the preface to the acknowledgements, I found *Nothing Is Wasted: A Memoir of God's Goodness in Every Season of Life* difficult to put down. David's story is every bit as inspirational as it is painful to imagine. His unwavering dependence on God's presence, even in the midst of unfathomable heartache and suffering, sustained him on his journey to healing, freedom, and purpose. His story is truly a gift, bringing hope to others seeking the same for their lives.

Andrew Jacobson
Chief Operating Officer, Crossmark Global Investments
Board Member, To Give A Smile

I first met David when his life was crazy. In fact, it was, as he mentioned in his writing, when he needed to switch from regular classes to the evening option. Since I was the director of the evening program he wanted to take advantage of, he needed acceptance through my office. The first time I saw him, with his right shoulder considerably lower than the left, and after hearing his reason for moving to evening classes, I was concerned about his ability to handle the workload required, given his demanding and unpredictable schedule. Well, he proved to be more than capable of accomplishing his academic objective in spite of the many challenges he faced. During our time together, I came to know him well and admire his commitment to God's calling on his life. We have kept in touch over the years since, and I'm still impressed with his passion for serving God and his compassion for others. He has become an inspiration to so many, including me. I pray you too will be encouraged and inspired through his writing.

George Filpansick
Former Professor & Director of Evening Program, Dallas Christian College

David Rose presents an open, genuine, and amazing testimonial in *Nothing Is Wasted*. He shares heart-breaking pain that he endured, both physical and mental. Yet through it all, David glorifies his Lord and Savior as he shows how God was able to redeem his past and continual trials to show God's love to so many others. Just as he has touched our lives by allowing God to work through him, we are sure you will be touched as well through David's resilient story of faith.

Dusty & Deb Sedars
Parents of a child impacted through the work of
To Give A Smile
Chapter Directors, To Give A Smile

This book is dedicated to my parents, Gary and Kelly; my siblings, Christina and Daniel; my family, my friends, and the countless doctors who have helped me to overcome one of life's toughest seasons.

I'm forever grateful for your support, wisdom, love, and encouragement.

CONTENTS

Foreword
by Ben Dailey

David Rose has a heart for people. Regardless of the title next to his name or the position he holds, his compassion for others influences every decision he makes. Whether he's resolving employee issues or has his hands deep in philanthropist work on the mission field, David always finds ways to pull potential out of any person he encounters and any situation he faces.

I have known David Rose for many years as his pastor. I've watched him lead in numerous situations in humility and astounding strength, never asking for or demanding the spotlight. He is a man of consistency and faithfulness, qualities that are rare in today's culture. David is generous—a true giver of his time, talents, and energy.

David's account of the challenges and obstacles he's navigated throughout his life is inspirational. From sexual abuse, bullying, and medical challenges to questioning his very purpose on earth, what understandably could have led to bitterness and defeat, David intentionally and purposefully chose to allow the Lord to turn into strength and success!

I don't know of a more qualified person to write on the

subject of nothing being wasted by God. David has not only witnessed but also experienced God, firsthand, redeem seasons that seemed completely stolen. David is a walking example of how God can turn around any situation and bring the absolute best out of it.

Perhaps you have walked through a season of sexual abuse or have been a victim of bullying and are feeling shame, defeat, or discouragement. Maybe you have spent a life filling your time with distractions so you don't have to deal with the pain. If you are walking through health challenges with no answers, or it seems like the current season will never end and you're exhausted, this book is for you. You'll be encouraged and empowered as you realize that God never wastes a season! There is a deep purpose in everything you walk through, and you are deeply loved beyond measure, even in the darkest moments of life.

Ben Dailey, Lead Pastor
Calvary Church and Network of Churches

Preface

Dear Reader,

I have been encouraged by many to share my story with the world. So many times, I started this journey of writing but would stop for whatever reason. Perhaps I wasn't ready to share some of my deepest hurts, frustrations, and trying moments with the world, or maybe life just got in the way. I believe that God has perfect timing for all things and has now given me the courage and the peace to share my story.

I am writing to encourage those who are being or have been abused, to tell them that they are not alone, and to remind them that they are individuals with value and purpose. I am writing to inspire those who are walking through medical-related needs to keep pressing forward and not to lose hope. I am writing to remind the kids who are being made fun of and bullied that they are perfectly and wonderfully made and that God has a perfect plan for each of them. I am writing to encourage parents watching their son or daughter face medical challenges to continue to cherish every moment while being reminded that God has never left them and is present in all seasons.

My prayer is that through this book, every reader will be

inspired never to give up. I pray that this book will bring encouragement, strength, and healing in your life and help you to release some of your deepest hurts by choosing to forgive those who have created wounds in your life. May you hold on to the truth that God can take the most deeply painful and trying times of our lives and turn them into something beautiful.

—David Rose

CHAPTER ONE

A Life-Changing Moment

I have made you and I will carry you; I will sustain you and I will rescue you.

—Isaiah 46:4 *(NIV)*

My parents began their special day, the day that marked their twenty-third wedding anniversary. This day that was meant to be set aside for celebration would later end in tragedy.

The weather in the small town of Defiance, Ohio, on October 24, 2003, was chilly and cloudy—no surprise for that time of year, with winter just a step around the corner. Nearly a thousand miles away, on the other hand, in the city of Dallas, Texas, the humidity was extremely high, and the temperature had soared well into the low nineties.

I had just completed another week of the hustle and bustle, running to and from class, late study nights, devos, and hang-out sessions, but there was no time to rest. I had to get to work. I quickly changed my hat from college student to shoe salesman and ran out the door.

As I got onto the freeway and headed to the mall where I worked, I hit the Dallas rush-hour traffic. Cars were bumper to bumper, and I thought, *"I'm going to be late!"* A sense of urgency flowed through my body as I maneuvered through the traffic to get to work. Thankfully, I arrived ten minutes before the clock-in time. I sighed in relief. In those few extra minutes, I took the opportunity to call my parents to wish them a happy anniversary.

"Hi, mom! Happy Anniversary!"

My mother replied, "Thanks, David. What are you doing?"

"I'm just about to walk into work. Do you all have any plans tonight to celebrate this special occasion?"

"Yes," my mom replied, "we are heading to Fort Wayne to have dinner and do some shopping."

"Oh, that sounds nice," I said, glancing down at my watch. "Well, I'd better be going. I will give you a call tomorrow. Hope you all have fun tonight. Love ya!"

"Love you, too. Have a good night at work and be careful driving home."

It seemed like the night would never end. The mall was completely dead. I kept trying to find things to keep me busy in the shoe department. Finally, after what seemed like days, the 9 p.m. closing time arrived. I had my cashier drawer counted and was ready to go.

A little after 9:30 p.m., the store manager gave me the clearance to leave, and boy, she did not have to tell me twice. I clocked out and darted to my car. It was Friday night, and I couldn't wait to get back to the dorms to see what all of my friends were up to. Dorm life never comes to an end, especially on weekends.

As I walked to my car, I felt the warm Texas air penetrating my inner core. I turned on my car, placed the A/C on full blast, and fastened my seat belt. Then I proceeded to the intersection and waited for the light to turn green. I looked ahead in a daze, tired and exhausted from a long week.

The arrow turned green, signifying that it was safe to turn across the six-lane intersection. I looked in both directions. Off to my left, there was a car stopped at the light in the lane closest to the curb while the lane next to it was unoccupied. I lightly touched the accelerator while turning the wheel counterclockwise.

My windows were rolled up, the radio playing softly, when suddenly I heard the sound of a car out of control, tires squealing, and what sounded like a driver struggling to regain control of a vehicle.

For a split second, I felt an adrenaline rush throughout my body as I desperately tried to locate the source of the noise to calm my worry. With a sense of desperation, I rapidly looked to my left, and all I saw were headlights beaming directly into my eyes. I froze, like a deer caught in headlights. My heart sank, and everything from that moment on happened in slow motion.

With no time to react, I felt a sense of helplessness and panic. Suddenly, I heard a voice, something indescribable, telling me to press the accelerator with all my might. I tensed up and gripped the steering wheel, holding on for dear life, as I floored the accelerator and said a quick prayer: *"God, please save me!"*

A tingling sensation trickled down my spine as I looked ahead.

A split second passed. Then all I heard was—BAM!

CHAPTER TWO

Stepping into Reality

For we are God's masterpiece. He has created us anew in Christ Jesus, so we can do the good things he planned for us long ago.

—Ephesians 2:10 *(NLT)*

Two Years Earlier

The concept of God knowing me before I was conceived in my mother's womb is unfathomable. It's difficult to grasp the thought of my Savior knowing me inside and out, not only what I would look like—my eye color, height, weight, and how many strands of hair I would have on my head—but also the issues with which I would struggle in my life, the lives I would impact for good or bad, what I would accomplish, and who I would become. God knew all of this before I was born.

I believe that throughout our lives, we are trying to find our purpose. We are searching for the meaning in our lives and what sets us apart from others. Why did God place us on this earth? What does He want each of us to achieve? That purpose comes early in life for some and later for others. It may come in a series of events, in dreams, in time spent with God in His Word, or through prayer. In my case, part of my calling and purpose was formed at an early age.

While a sophomore in high school, I attended a youth conference in Denver, Colorado. One evening, I was asked to walk through the stadium and pray for the students who would be attending in less than an hour. Those involved were praying for anointing over the students and that God would release the chains binding them, the burdens and dead weight, and speak to them that evening. After our prayer, the doors opened, and in poured thousands of students from all over the country.

During the powerful praise and worship, I looked around to see students of all ages singing and praising God's name, a view that I found breathtaking, upbeat, and glorious. Thousands of students were laying their burdens, heavy weights, frustrations, and disappointments at the foot of the cross as they sang, "Here I am. Take me as an offering...."[1]

As I stood there and observed, I wanted more of God. At the same time, I was frustrated about things that had occurred in my life. I began to sing, "Lord, here I am. Take me as an offering," and I surrendered to Him. In that moment, God's presence spoke to me as He began to plant the seed of a vision within me.

To this day, I can't remember who spoke that evening's message, but he used an illustration that I will never forget. It continues to remind me that the world is both simple and complex and how the struggles that we face can cloud our judgment, overcome our mindset, and consume us if we allow them to do so.

The speaker took two bottles and placed them on a table so the entire audience could see them. One of the bottles was full of golf balls, and the other was empty. The bottles were an illustration of our lives while the golf balls symbolized the dead weight, emotions, and baggage people often carry with them throughout their lives.

The speaker began pouring sand into both containers a little at a time. The sand symbolized our life moments, inner joy, peace, and happiness. As you may imagine, the container holding the golf balls overflowed quickly. On the other hand, the empty bottle had room for more sand, signifying that an unburdened heart is more open to receiving the opportunities and blessings that God pours into each of our lives. The heart that doesn't hold on to emotional baggage can be happy, content, and full of joy.

This simple illustration put life's chaos and unseen matters of the soul into perspective. It helped me to see that life is worth living and that Christians ought to let go of the frustration, pain, and bitterness that is filling them up and surrender their lives fully to God so that they can be free to seek their divine purpose and step into the role God wills them to fulfill.

In that moment, I realized that my life was becoming like the bottle full of golf balls. As a young teenager, I had built up so much inner frustration. I was full of past hurts that I didn't know how to deal with properly or communicate to anyone. This pain and frustration were crowding out my inner joy and keeping me from being happy.

Throughout my childhood years, my dad held the role of a bi-vocational pastor, meaning that he worked a full-time job while pastoring a church. The congregation we were a part of envisioned growing, but every time new people came through our doors, they were run off for some reason or another by those who had started the church. My dad faithfully served, pouring himself into others, but seldom did they express that same love and encouragement toward our family. I learned quickly how to put on a mask and pretend that all was well while inwardly I was becoming more frustrated and confused. The church body was supposed to be the true light and to show the love of Jesus but was instead doing the complete opposite.

In school, I just wanted to fit in, but I was more of an outcast and the kid who was made fun of. Deep down, I dreaded school—not so much the studying and classwork, but the social pressure to be accepted. The harsh words others spoke to me became deeply rooted within me. I suppressed my feelings and became less confident about who I was.

Below all of the mess, I carried a deep secret that not a single other person in my life knew. So often, I wanted to release it and tell someone, but I just didn't know how. When I was six years old, the father of my best friend at the time began abusing me sexually. I initially thought that it was something that every child went through, a part of the growing-up process. As the years progressed, it not only continued, but became more intense. In my mid-teens, I began to piece together that what I was going through wasn't normal, and I stopped the abuse, but the damage had already been done. Deep down, I thought that maybe I had done something to bring it on.

Inwardly, I was broken, insecure, and hurt. I questioned God and why all of this had happened to me. I hid behind layers of masks and various coping mechanisms while outwardly pretending that my life was put together. I was exhausted and tired of trying to carry the burdens on my own. As I prayed that evening, I asked God to show me how to release the baggage, deadweight, and emotions of my past, but little did I know that it would take time and other people He would place in my life to help heal those wounds.

During that time, God revealed a part of my calling here on earth. He laid on my heart to become a motivational speaker and share the message of hope, the message that no matter what your past is, who you once were, and who you currently are, God loves, He saves, He provides, He comforts, and He heals.

Walking back to my hotel room that evening, I was in complete silence. I knew that God could use the bad and the ugly and turn it all into something beautiful, but I didn't know how or when. I went on to pray, *"Okay, God, You revealed a calling to me, and that is great and all, but I don't have much of a testimony. There are other people who have been through far more than I have. Why would anyone listen to me?"*

The scripture that came to mind was Jeremiah 1:5:

"Before I formed you in the womb I knew you, before you were born I set you apart" (NIV). God was in control of my life, and that was all that mattered. He had set me apart, just as He does all of His other children. I returned home, and the calling remained on my mind. As I continued on with my life, I prayerfully sought direction and guidance as to how to deal with the past and when my calling and ministry would begin.

CHAPTER THREE

Senior Year

"For I know the plans I have for you," declares the LORD,
"plans to prosper you and not to harm you, plans to give
you hope and a future."
—Jeremiah 29:11 *(NIV)*

Before I knew it, I was a senior in high school. I had waited
so long for this year to come, longing for the day when I could
be called a senior.

The class year began on a hot summer morning at band
camp. All of the marching band students, myself among
them, were out learning the new songs and routines for the
upcoming season. I realized then that the title "senior" carried
more weight than I had anticipated. So many students were
looking up to me and the rest of the seniors for direction,
especially the freshmen, who were new to all of this. My
sister, Christina, was part of the freshman group, and I was
excited to show her the ropes, just as my brother, Daniel, had
done when he was a senior and I was a freshman.

In the coming months, every Friday night, we were out at the football games, laughing and cutting up in between our songs and performing the halftime shows. I have to admit that I enjoyed being in the position of a senior. I liked knowing that the hardest part of my education was behind me, and I also appreciated being in a position of influence. I could help younger students to make wise decisions and encourage them that before long they would be in the same position I was.

Because I was ahead of the credits needed to graduate, I had the option to take additional classes, either at the school or at a nearby college, or to work a job that would report back to my school on hours obtained. I had recently started a part-time job at JCPenney, working evenings to help save money for college, so I decided to check to see if I could pick up additional hours. I was reliable and hard-working, and they gladly accepted me to work part of the day while keeping my hours in the evening. It seemed perfect, only having to go to school for half a day and then going to work at the store. I had applied so much effort over the years to maintain good grades that I just wanted to have a break and enjoy less of a load before going off to college.

My senior year was going well until I got a message from a friend of mine that one of my close friends, Alexandra, had been rushed to a hospital in Fort Wayne, Indiana. Both Alex and her mom were close to our family. I hurried in to tell my parents. Shortly afterwards, my mom and I dropped everything and drove to the hospital, which was about an hour away from Defiance.

Upon our arrival, we were greeted in the waiting room by Alex's mother, Betty, and she informed us that Alex had just been taken to surgery. Minutes seemed to pass by like hours, and hours seemed like eternity. I stared and stared at the dark-blue carpet, which had white specks in a unique pattern, as I wondered about her fate.

After two-and-a-half long hours, the doctor finally walked down the well-lit hallway. We immediately jumped to our feet, joyful and also fearful of the unknown words we were about to hear.

"She pulled through, and we took care of the problem just in time, before it turned fatal. Everything seems to be okay, but there is still a chance of complications," the doctor told us.

Relief filled the room. My mom and I hugged Betty and told her that we would be thinking of and praying for all of them, and we asked her to keep us posted. Then my mom and I headed back home, as it was already late in the evening on Sunday and we both had to be up early the next morning.

After school on Monday, I called Alex's mom and asked how she was doing. She informed me that she was doing much better. I continued to touch base daily to check if Alex was improving. By Wednesday, I was informed that she had been released from the hospital. I was so happy to hear it!

Over the following weekend, my family and I headed down to Dayton to visit my grandparents and other extended family. It was always good to see them, and I cherished the times when we went to visit. They were a good three-hour drive from us, so we were not able to visit as much as I would have liked.

When we returned home, I noticed that the answering machine was flashing. When I played it, I found out that Alex had taken a turn for the worse and had to be hospitalized.

Once again, my mom and I were on our way to the hospital to give support. When we arrived, Alex had been asking for me, so I was able to go to the pediatric intensive care unit.

When I entered the room, Alex seemed to be awake. She rose slightly in her bed and said, "David..."

Her voice faded. Her face was pale, white as snow, and she lay motionless after the sudden jolt to greet me.

"David, I can't stand the pain in my head anymore."

I knew that she was referring to her headaches, which were caused by a condition in which excess cerebrospinal fluid collected in her brain's ventricles.[2]

"Hang in there, Alex," I said encouragingly. "You're going to get through this. We're praying for you!"

Shortly after that, Alex was once again wheeled back to surgery. As I watched her being taken down the hallway, I wondered if I would ever see her again. Her condition had become so critical that her fate was unknown.

Within a few hours, the surgery was completed and was a success. *"Thank God,"* I thought. The shunt in her head that the doctors had to replace the first time needed to be repositioned because it wasn't working properly.

My mom and I headed back home a few hours after the procedure. On our way, I struck up a conversation with her. I had seen different stories on television of remarkable young kids who continued to keep a positive attitude despite all that they were going through in terms of health issues.

"Mom," I said, "if I ever face any health issues, I want to be someone who keeps a positive attitude and inspires others."

"David, you never know what God has in store for your life. You are always so caring and want the best for others. You maintain such a good attitude, and that is the key to life. I'm proud of you! I'm proud of the friend you have been to Alex and the support you have given her. She needed that."

"Thanks, Mom. I appreciate you coming along with me."

In the coming weeks, Alex returned home and was doing much better. Gradually, she got back into school and caught up with her classes.

I thought a lot about that experience in the days ahead and how tomorrow is never promised. I had always had a big, caring heart, and I started to consider what career path I might want to embark on. I had always wanted to be a doctor and care for the sick, but I began to realize that I didn't have the stomach for being a doctor. Any sight of blood made me feel nauseous. The final straw was when my anatomy class took a tour of the University of Toledo Medical Center, including a visit to the morgue. As the instructor started opening a body and pulling out different organs to show us, I became very weak and felt like I was about to pass out. I excused myself and went out into the hallway until they were finished.

From that moment onward, I decided that being a doctor or anesthesiologist wasn't for me. I continued to pray for direction while bouncing around ideas of different colleges I might attend and career paths I might want to pursue. One day, one of my fellow students interviewed me for the senior yearbook and asked me what I wanted to do with my life. *"Such a big question,"* I thought.

The more I considered it, the more I thought that working in some type of industry that gave back to the community, especially caring for the sick, would be something that I would enjoy. I had a heart for people, which became all that much clearer to me through the recent situation with Alex. Therefore, I replied that working for a nonprofit, such as Make-A-Wish, while being a motivational speaker would be something that would interest me.

The interviewer replied, "I can see that, David."

In the following months, I continued applying to different colleges. With all that I had gone through with the abuse, I really wanted to get away from the small town and, for that matter, the state of Ohio. I envisioned myself living in a big city and felt that it was important to attend a Christian university or college.

Before long, I was walking down the aisle in the gymnasium at my local school. Graduation day had arrived! I had chosen to attend Dallas Christian College and to go the route of business administration because I thought that would allow me to get a good education that I could apply to any industry.

I had dreamed for so long of what the future would hold. As I walked up to receive my diploma, I knew that God had something marvelous in store for me.

CHAPTER FOUR

New Surroundings

Be very careful, then, how you live—not as unwise but as wise, making the most of every opportunity, because the days are evil.
—Ephesians 5:15–16 *(NIV)*

On a warm, muggy day in mid-August, I boarded a plane in Dayton, Ohio, bound for the big city of Dallas, Texas, leaving behind the world that I had always known. A part of me was ready to move on and forget all of the pain and frustration of my past while another side was reluctant to leave the family I loved. Any college student who is particularly close to his or her family can relate to how difficult it is to say goodbye to loved ones.

I hugged my mother, sister, and father and was walking through the security line when I saw my mom and sister burst into tears. I felt like my heart was being ripped out of my chest. My first impulse was to run and take both of them into my arms and tell them that it was going to be okay. But was it? Would I be able to be that far away from family? What challenges and obstacles would I face in the days ahead? I proceeded through the security checkpoint, waving to them but feeling deeply saddened. I reminded myself that I would be back to visit before long. I tried to keep a positive attitude even though I had no idea what the next chapter in my life would hold.

Upon arriving at Dallas/Fort Worth International Airport, I stepped off the plane and proceeded to baggage claim to retrieve my items. I began browsing the crowd, trying to find someone who appeared to be looking for a person he had never met. My roommate and I had talked all but three days before I was scheduled to arrive in Texas. Neither of us had a clue what the other looked like, as this was before social media became widely available. Of course, we couldn't take the fun out of it!

Out of the blue, I heard someone come up behind me and say, "Are you David?"

I turned and saw the speaker reaching out his hand like he knew for sure that I was the young man he had recently spoken to on the phone. The blank look I had on my face must have given me away. Likewise, I reached out my hand and said, "Paul, nice to meet you."

I spotted my bags and lugged them off the belt before we proceeded to his truck. While driving back to the dorms, Paul asked me if I was a basketball fan. Of course, I said, "Yeah," even though it wasn't a sport that I lived and breathed. I could tell that Paul was a hardcore San Antonio Spurs fan. He started talking about all of the players as well as the NBA titles that the team had won. It was cool to hear him share his passion, and I smiled to myself.

When we arrived at the college, Paul and I headed in to find our dorm room. *"Home sweet home,"* I thought as I began to unpack my bags.

Not long after getting all settled in the room, Paul and I went with a friend of his from San Antonio who was also attending the college to grab something to eat at a nearby restaurant. Afterwards, we did a little exploring around the city and the campus since it was all new to us.

Later that evening, I came across the following scripture: "Be very careful, then, how you live—not as unwise but as wise, making the most of every opportunity, because the days are evil" (Ephesians 5:15–16 NIV). As I lay down, I thought, *"God has led me here to this college. Now I need to step back, trust in Him, and make the best of what lies ahead."*

CHAPTER FIVE

Every Parent's Worst Nightmare

*Do not be anxious about anything, but in every situation,
by prayer and petition, with thanksgiving, present your
requests to God.*
—Philippians 4:6 *(NIV)*

The first day of college was very intimidating. Being in an
unfamiliar city on a new campus and not knowing a soul was
a bit hard to take in. I felt sick to my stomach, and every part
of me wanted to turn back, throw up my hands, and say,
"This is not for me!"

Lying in bed that evening, I felt numb and homesick, but
my brain was telling me that I was not a quitter. To every
project, every task, and every journey given to me, I always
gave one hundred percent. My brain and heart needed to be
in alignment. God had led me and placed me, and He was
going to use me in this new location. I found comfort and
encouragement in the following scripture: "Do not be
anxious about anything, but in every situation, by prayer and

petition, with thanksgiving, present your requests to God" (Philippians 4:6 NIV). I knew that I had to place my trust in Him, knowing that He would give me the calmness, the guidance, and the perseverance I would need to "do all things through Christ who strengthens me" (Philippians 4:13 NKJV).

When my heart and mind aligned, I determined that there was no turning back, the homesickness subsided, and time began flying by. Before long, I was preparing for my midterm exams. I had multiple late-night cramming sessions and was constantly pumping caffeine into my system to stay awake. The motivation to keep going through the long week was a four-day weekend with my family after the midterm exams. I could not wait! I had not been home since classes started.

On a Friday morning in mid-October, I flew out of my bed. Nothing could get in the way of me going home to see my family. Upon completion of my last exam, I was off to the airport to begin the journey back home. Once I arrived in Fort Wayne, Indiana, after what seemed like forever, I proceeded down the escalators in the airport, and there stood my family. It was so good to see them! Joy overcame me, and a huge smile filled my face as I ran up to them and gave them a big hug.

We packed my bags into the car and headed off to eat at one of my favorite restaurants, Carlos O'Kelly's in the Fort Wayne area. I knew that I would have a long weekend of being spoiled, and I was going to soak it all in as much as I possibly could. After eating, we made a few stops at various stores prior to starting the one-hour journey back to my hometown of Defiance, Ohio.

I spent the weekend catching up with my friends, having late-night conversations with my sister and cookouts with the family, and being surrounded by those who loved me. I could not have asked for a better weekend.

Tuesday morning came around. My time at home had gone excessively fast. However, I knew that the Thanksgiving break was only a few weeks away, and I would be back to celebrate the holiday with my family. As I said goodbye in the airport later that morning, the thought of not seeing my family again never crossed my mind.

When classes and my busy schedule resumed on Wednesday, I felt refreshed, rejuvenated, and prepared to plow through the two months remaining of the fall semester.

Two Weeks Later

> He performs wonders that cannot be fathomed, miracles that cannot be counted.
> —*Job 5:9* (NIV)

On the evening of October 24, 2003, back home in Defiance, Ohio, my parents had just gotten back from their anniversary dinner. My mother felt restless and uneasy as she got ready for bed, but she could not quite put her finger on what was causing the worry. She said her evening prayers and immediately crawled into bed, thinking that her anxiety might have been from the everyday worries of life. She closed her eyes and tried to shift her thoughts elsewhere.

23

In Dallas, shortly after 9:50 p.m., fear and adrenaline pumped through my body as headlights beamed directly into my eyes. Flooring the accelerator, acting in faith, I looked straight ahead instead of in the direction from which the car was coming. I tensed in this moment of uncertainty and prayed desperately, *"God, please save me!"*

Every part of my body was clinging to hope that the last-minute push of the accelerator was enough to avoid the collision. A tingling sensation trickled down my spine as I looked ahead, waiting.

Nearly a second had passed, and I thought that I was in the clear when suddenly—*bam!*—the sound of metal hitting metal. My heart sank in pure disappointment. I closed my eyes and held on for dear life.

I did not recall much after that moment. I am not sure if I blacked out for a period of time or if I simply didn't want to face reality. When I again became aware of my surroundings, I opened my eyes. I had no idea what to expect with regard to the shape of the vehicle or, more importantly, my body was in. I noticed right off that I was looking in the same direction as I had been looking prior to the collision. I then looked down, hopeful, and from what I could tell, my limbs and legs were still moving. There were no signs of blood. I thought, *"Praise God! Praise God! My prayers were answered. I'm still alive!"*

I was right in the middle of the intersection, so I decided to drive the vehicle to the parking lot that was off to the side of the road to avoid any further collisions. The driver of the other vehicle was nowhere in sight.

Witnesses in the Burger King parking lot could not believe what they had just observed. A vehicle out of control, traveling between 60 and 80 miles per hour, clipped the back end of my car, putting me into a 360-degree spin. Miraculously, I walked away from the accident without a scratch on me.

Still in shock and disbelief over what had just happened, tense and shaken up, I quickly called my mom for comfort. When she picked up, she sounded groggy, which meant that I had woken her up.

"Mom, I was in a pretty bad accident, but I'm okay." My voice was a bit shaky, and my lip was quivering, so she could tell that I wasn't truly okay. I might have been physically unhurt, but I was mentally and emotionally shaken. "I needed to call and let you know. Police are on their way."

My mother, like any other concerned parent, said, "Honey, are you sure you are okay? Maybe you should go to the hospital." Her voice was cracking.

Knowing that she was about to start crying, I replied, "No, I'm okay. I just wanted to let you know what happened. I will call you back shortly."

Police arrived, took my statement, and asked if I needed an ambulance. I felt fine at the time, jolted but okay, so I said no. I decided to attempt to drive back to the dorm in the beat-up car since the dorm was only a few miles from the crash location.

Once I arrived, I felt the safety net and security of home surround me, and I sighed in relief. All of the stresses of dealing with the car, the insurance, and so forth flooded my mind, but they were the least of my worries. Shortly after I got to my room, the pain started to set in. I thought that it was related to whiplash, so I took some Tylenol and didn't think much of it. Afterwards, I knew that I needed to call my mom to let her know that her son was home safely. We conversed for a few brief minutes before I told her that I loved her and would connect with her sometime in the morning.

In my heart, I knew that God had performed an incredible miracle and saved my life. I thanked Him in my prayers and drifted off to sleep.

CHAPTER SIX

Aftermath

Rejoice always, pray continually, give thanks in all circumstances; for this is God's will for you in Christ Jesus.
—1 Thessalonians 5:16–18 *(NIV)*

I woke up in the wee hours of the morning in a good amount of discomfort that began at the base of my skull and carried down my neck to my upper extremities. At the time, I assumed that the discomfort was from the whiplash that I suffered during the direct impact of the collision and sudden jolt of the car spinning out of control. I took additional medicine, but nothing seemed to help relieve the pain and the tingling sensation that I had going down my neck.

In the morning, after not getting much sleep, I called my family for consultation to see whether they recommended that I go to the emergency room. Being the stubborn person I was, I debated whether to give it more time or to go to a local ER to have everything checked out.

As I assumed, my mother said, "Honey, I really think that

you need to go to the hospital to ensure that you haven't suffered any internal damage."

"I know," I responded, even though I was still thinking in the back of my mind that I should give it more time.

After much debate and consultation with my parents, I decided to go to a local ER. I proceeded through the double sliding-glass doors, knowing that my heavenly Father was with me.

As I sat in the emergency room alone, my mind drifted back to the last time I was a patient in a hospital, at the age of five. My family and I were living out in Woonsocket, South Dakota, a small, secluded town in the southeast part of the state. My parents had surprised us kids and taken us to our first live rodeo a few hours away in the larger city of Sioux Falls. I had watched a few rodeos on television before, but this was my first time watching a rodeo live, with all of the action taking place directly in front of me.

We arrived at the rodeo grounds and took our places in the bleachers. I could hardly hold back my excitement! It was the first big event we were attending as a family.

Before long, the rodeo began. Everywhere I turned, there was so much action constantly taking place. I had always been a big horse fan, and for a brief second, I felt like I was in heaven. I was in the world I loved. A good thirty minutes into the excitement, the announcer came over the intercom and got the crowd enthused about the next big event, bull riding, eight seconds of man against beast.

It happened suddenly. One moment, I was sitting with my family, and the next, I was lying on the ground, looking directly up at the bleachers. I had scooted up a little too much and fallen a good two to three stories to the ground beneath me.

I didn't fully know what was going on. I tried to stand but heard my mom yell, "Don't get up! Just stay there!" I lay back down on the ground.

Shortly thereafter, people surrounded me. My parents were there, trying to comfort me and telling me to lie still.

"Everything is going to be okay," my dad said.

Paramedics arrived and quickly strapped me to a stretcher. The EMTs asked if I wanted my mother or father to go with me in the ambulance. I chose my father because I thought that he would be the best person to handle the situation calmly.

When we arrived at the hospital, I was taken into the emergency room. Things happened quickly from the time of my arrival. The ER doctor did a thorough exam, followed by a series of X-rays. After several hours, my parents were informed that I was just fine. Based on their evaluation, I had no internal bleeding or broken bones. I was released from the hospital later that evening.

My parents were later informed by ground crew and paramedics that based on where I fell, I was less than an inch from falling directly into the support beams. I was a walking miracle.

As I sat in the emergency room all those years later, I realized that God had prevented my second big accident from being worse than it could have been. After a little over an hour and a half of waiting, my name was announced, and I proceeded back to the examining room. The doctor walked in shortly afterwards and took down my statement regarding the accident, the approximate time it had occurred, the location, and how it had happened. He briefly examined me, and I assume that he determined the pain was due to whiplash. He prescribed painkillers and muscle relaxers, and he referred me to a local doctor for a follow-up appointment. No X-rays or extensive evaluations were conducted.

On Monday, I met with the family physician I was referred to, there in Dallas, Dr. Dodge, who prescribed additional medicine and physical therapy. Two days later, the physical therapy rehab center at the local hospital conducted a thorough evaluation of my injuries and limitations, which lasted a good forty-five minutes. The therapist then had me lie flat on a bed and placed electrode pads on my neck and upper extremities that fired and released electrical stimulation to help loosen and relax the tense muscles in my neck.

That evening, I lay in bed in a great deal of agony. It was difficult to stay focused on my studies due to the pain and constant annoyance of the tingling sensation down my neck. I never knew that whiplash could cause such an extreme amount of discomfort at the base of the skull and in the neck and shoulder areas. I thought, *"I hope that the doctors are not missing something here."*

My next follow-up appointment fell on the following Monday. The physical therapist began with several exercises to loosen the muscles, followed by additional electrical stimulation. After the fifteen-minute stimulation, the physical therapist said, "Before you go, let's have you work on strengthening the muscles in your arms for a little bit."

I thought, *"Sure. Why not? My slim, scrawny body could use some muscle tone."*

The therapist reviewed the exercises with me, handed over the five-pound weights, and went on to instruct another patient as I continued with the exercises he had shown me. I was looking out at the parking lot through the glass windows, with my back turned to the therapist. From a distance, he noticed that my body was not aligned. He walked up to me and instructed me to put the weights down and stand up straight. There was concern in his voice when he said, "Your right thoracic region is significantly lower than your left thoracic area."

I thought, *"What is he talking about? I mean, really?"* My shoulders had always been straight, so in the back of my mind, I blew him off. I'm sure that my facial expression reflected my thoughts.

The physical therapist then stated, "I need you to follow up with your referring doctor immediately." Concern entered my mind with the word *immediately*. I knew that couldn't be good. The physical therapist went on to say that he wanted to halt any therapy appointments that I had scheduled until there was clear insight into what was going on internally so we could avoid causing further damage.

As I approached my car, the first thing I did was look at my reflection in the car window to see if I could notice any decrease in my right thoracic area. Sure enough, my right thoracic area seemed to be a bit lower than the left. I took a moment to call my doctor's office to see when the next available appointment would be. The receptionist stated that she had an opening at 2 p.m. the next day. I had a college class at that time, but I knew that I needed to take the appointment despite the scheduling conflict.

I waited anxiously. It seemed like 2 p.m. would never come. I wanted to know what was going on with my body right then and there, what the next steps were, and what the course of treatment for my injuries would be. Little did I know at the time that an answer to these questions would be miles away.

When my appointment finally came, Dr. Dodge re-examined my body and asked, "What happened?" He noticed the decrease and weakness in the right thoracic area, which was not present when he initially examined my body a week prior. Dr. Dodge seemed concerned, but he held his composure and said, "Let me make a quick call, and I will be back in here in just a moment."

When he returned to the examining room, Dr. Dodge told me that he was referring me to a sports medicine facility that had multiple doctors who specialized in orthopedics and spine care. He said, "I have consulted with an orthopedic surgeon and made you an appointment today for 4:45 p.m., as I believe this is an injury that needs to be looked at as soon as possible."

Looking down at my watch, I realized that it was nearly 3:15 p.m., which meant that I had only an hour and a half to find the doctor's office to which he was referring me. Being new to Dallas, I had no clue how to get from point A to point

B and which roads and highways intersected. This was before GPS units became common.

The receptionist handed me a map and walked me step by step through the instructions for how to get to the facility. The medical building was a good forty-five-minute drive from my current location. I quickly hurried to my car, studying the map thoroughly.

As I began driving to the doctor's office, I prayed for protection and safety, and a resounding peace came over me that everything was going to be okay. After forty minutes of driving, I began to think that maybe I had missed my turn. It seemed like I was getting further away from any commercial areas. I recalled the receptionist saying, "You will eventually pass railroad tracks, and once you do, there will be an open field with cows grazing. Eventually, on your right, will be the sports medicine facility." I continued to drive down Josey Lane until I saw railroad tracks. Just as the receptionist had described, there sat the building.

When I pulled into the doctor's office parking lot, I looked down at the clock in my car and realized that I was twenty minutes early. I took the opportunity to call my mom to keep her in the loop regarding the events that had taken place throughout the afternoon. I assumed with it being shortly after 5 p.m. Ohio time that her school-bus route had ended for the day. As soon as I placed the call, my mother's voice gave me a residing comfort and reassured me that everything was going to be okay.

Dr. Graehl, the orthopedic surgeon to whom I was referred, was the first specialist I saw regarding my injuries.

He had taken the call less than two hours ago from my primary-care doctor. As he walked into the examining room, he extended his hand to shake mine. He explained that he had spoken to Dr. Dodge at great length regarding my case. Dr. Graehl admitted right off that he was the only doctor available within the office that evening. He specialized in hip and knee reconstructive surgery, but due to the sense of urgency, he agreed to examine me and would pass the information along to the doctor in whose care I would be once he returned from his vacation.

The doctor proceeded to examine my arm and shoulder, and he ordered several X-rays and additional testing. Once the results were back, Dr. Graehl reviewed the reports. He did not see any structural damage that would explain the drooped right thoracic region, so he assumed that it was a nerve injury. He informed me that he would have an extensive conversation with the spine specialist in the office building once he returned from his vacation, and he instructed the nurse to schedule an appointment for me for the coming Thursday, when the doctor would be back in the office.

Walking out of the building, I felt a sense of disappointment and frustration. I had not yet received any answers that would explain my pain and other symptoms.

I called my mom from my car in the parking lot of the medical building and told her what Dr. Graehl had said to me. From the tone of my voice, she could sense the disappointment, frustration, and uncertainty that were building up within me. She tried to comfort me, saying,

"David, it is all going to be okay. Hang in there."

When I got back to my dorm, my mom called to tell me that she had booked a flight to arrive tomorrow night around midnight into Dallas/Fort Worth International Airport. A part of me felt relieved even though I was trying so hard to be strong and pretend that I could handle the news by myself. My mother would not take "no" for an answer. She said, "I will see you tomorrow night."

Little did I know that my symptoms would get progressively worse. By morning, the right trapezius muscle, which helps to support the scapula and the arm, had weakened significantly. As a result, there was decreased movement, and discoloration had set in. My left shoulder was much higher than normal, presumably because my body was overcompensating to support the right side. When I forced my left shoulder down into a normal position, my left arm would turn cold and take on a dark, purplish tint. My inner voice was screaming, *"What is happening?"*

Around 12:20 a.m., my mom walked through the circular, spinning glass doors at DFW International Airport. Her smile and presence gave me the reassurance I needed that everything was going to be okay. She walked up to me, holding back her tears, and gave me a kiss and a hug. She held me tightly in her arms for a few minutes, a gesture that both of us needed. In that moment, I knew that I had a support system that was going to fight the battle with me no matter how long it would take, the obstacles we would encounter, and the disappointments we would face.

The Next Morning

On that November morning, the temperature was hovering in the low seventies as my mom and I drove to the medical building in Carrolton, Texas. Since the accident, my surroundings had changed. The leaves had begun to turn colors, and the temperature had started to break from the upper eighties to a more comfortable upper seventies. Thanksgiving break was only a week away.

As we drove to the clinic, the following scripture came to mind:

Rejoice always, pray continually, give thanks in all circumstances; for this is God's will for you in Christ Jesus.
—*1 Thessalonians 5:16–18 (NIV)*

I couldn't explain why this particular circumstance was happening to me. I didn't know how long the journey would take or what the end result would be, but I knew that God was going to be with me.

Dr. Frazier, a spine specialist, joined my mother and me in the examining room shortly after 10 a.m. He introduced himself and conducted a thorough examination of my injuries, limitations, and structural appearance. Afterwards, he ordered a whole bunch of X-rays that he reviewed there in the examining room. He concluded that the weakness in the right thoracic area was likely a result of nerve damage.

Unfortunately, he went on to say that the only way to conclude whether or not nerve damage was present was to run an electromyogram, also known as an EMG study. This test is not recommended to be completed until three to four weeks after the initial injury because nerves can continue to fire off signals, giving inaccurate readings. The doctor suggested conducting the study the first week of December, which would be exactly three weeks from the time the shoulder had dropped.

Before Dr. Frazier could provide additional information, my mother asked, "What do we do if the left thoracic area suddenly begins to drop?"

He replied, "What do you mean by 'begins to drop'?"

My mother clarified, "Well, his right thoracic area just started to drop more than a week after the accident. What will prevent the other thoracic area from doing the same?"

Dr. Frazier's demeanor and facial expression shifted from calmness to concern. He flipped through the records the nurse had handed to him and said, "So, if I'm hearing you correctly, the thoracic area began to weaken a week ago, not immediately after the accident."

My mother, with a concerned look on her face, replied, "Yes, that is correct."

The specialist called in the nurse, and he re-evaluated my neck, arm, and trapezius muscle area. "I need a stat MRI run on Mr. Rose today, if at all possible, for the brain, thoracic, lumbar, and brachial plexus area, and let me know how soon any facility here in Dallas can get him in." He then turned to my mother and me and explained that the course he was planning to take had changed now that he knew that the weakness had just started. He said, "I have ordered all four

MRIs to see if there is any structural damage that might have caused the sudden weakness to occur. Based on the results, we'll know more at that time."

Looking over at my mother, I could see the worry written all over her face. The doctor must have sensed it as well, because he offered to pray with us while we sat in the examining room. I was thrilled to know that God had placed a Christian physician in our lives to lead and direct us from a medical standpoint during this uncertain time.

A little over two hours later, I was lying in the enclosed MRI machine. I felt imprisoned, lifeless, and claustrophobic. A brace was placed on my neck and shoulder to prevent any movement in the area they were imaging. I felt like I was about to lose my mind from being in such tight quarters and not being able to move or get out of the machine. Headphones were placed on my ears so I could listen to music to help comfort me and take my mind off what was happening around me. The radiologist nurse who was conducting the imaging advised me that she was about to start the MRI, which would take about two-and-a-half hours or more.

"Two-and-a-half hours!" I thought. *"No wonder she waited until I was in the machine and completely strapped to the bed to spring this on me!"* I didn't think that I would be able to endure a few minutes in this claustrophobic environment, let alone two-and-a-half hours.

"Okay, we are about to begin the test. Are you doing okay?" the radiologist nurse asked through the microphone.

"No, not really," I thought, but I went ahead and said,

"Yes." I realized early on in the process that in order to get well, I needed to do whatever it took to take my mind off what was happening around me and put my survival hat on. I shifted my thoughts to reliving good memories, such as family vacations. I prayed, listened to Christian music, and reviewed my mental weekly task list to distract myself from what was taking place.

From time to time, the radiologist nurse would check in on me, which gave me a break from the annoying knocking and pounding noises from the machine. A little more than two-and-a-half hours later, the nurse told me that she was all done. I was glad to get that over with and to be one step closer to answers.

CHAPTER SEVEN

Taking Health for Granted

The eternal God is your refuge, and his everlasting arms are under you.
                                        —Deuteronomy 33:27 *(NLT)*

Thursday finally arrived, the day I was scheduled to meet with Dr. Frazier to review the MRIs. I was prepared for results. Shortly after I arrived at the clinic, the doctor walked into the examining room. He looked at my mom and me as he reviewed the MRIs and said that all four reports showed negative results. No structural damage appeared on the imaging that would explain my injuries. The doctor believed that the EMG study would provide further clarity, but we would need to wait another two weeks to run this test.

Being the positive, optimistic person I was, I put a smile on my face and reminded myself not to be anxious, but to give everything to God in prayer, even though I desperately wanted answers.

The next day, I said goodbye for now to my mom as she

boarded a plane to head back to Ohio. Deep down, it was difficult to see her leave, but outwardly I maintained a confident attitude that I was going to be just fine.

In the days ahead, my symptoms continued to get worse. My right thoracic region kept falling lower and lower while my left thoracic region was being carried higher than normal, resulting in an eight- to nine-inch difference between my shoulders! The imbalance started to have a significant impact on my circulatory system, heart, and spinal cord, which resulted in decreased functionality and balance.

I would often wake up in the middle of the night with no function in my right arm. It would be completely numb and lifeless. Fear captivated my mind, and I would have to use my left arm to reposition what seemed like dead weight. Each time this happened, I wondered whether I would ever regain function again. At times, it would take up to thirty minutes for me to be able to move my right arm fully. I thought, *"What's happening? What are the doctors missing?"*

Ten Days Later

Tuesday, December 2, was the big day. I was excited because I was turning 19 and also believed that I would find answers to my condition at my follow-up appointment that afternoon. Around 2 p.m., I was lying on the exam-room table as the doctor began to conduct the electromyography test. After multiple hours of poking a needle into my neck, upper back, and thoracic region, the specialist told me that he did not see any nerves that were showing a weakened signal response that would explain my condition. He reassured me that we were going to get to the bottom of this. He would conduct additional research to see what other diagnoses might make sense given my symptoms before proceeding with additional testing. Prior to my leaving, the doctor ordered a large amount of blood work and stated that he would review those results and begin ruling out any other possibilities of diseases or conditions that he was considering.

When I returned to my dorm room shortly after 7 p.m., I was silent, at a loss for words, as I sat in the room, staring at the wall. I was so discouraged, frustrated, and confused as to why all of this was happening. My roommate, Paul, walked in, and he could tell that I wasn't my typical self. He asked how the appointment had gone earlier that day, and I told him that I had been at the doctor's office all afternoon and had walked out with no more information than I had gone in with. Knowing that I needed to take my mind off everything, he asked me if I wanted to go grab some food with some friends.

I responded, "Thanks, but I think I'm going to stay in tonight." I didn't want to tell him that, deep down, I just wasn't in the mood to carry on a conversation.

An hour or so had passed when I heard a knock at the door. I opened it, and in walked Paul and several of our friends, holding a birthday cake lit up with candles and singing "Happy Birthday." For the first time in the thirty-nine days since the accident had occurred, I was present and enjoying the moment. My mind shifted from the pain I was experiencing and the ongoing uncertainty of my health to being a college student and hanging with my buddies. Looking back, I can see that this small gesture was the medicine I needed to help prepare me for the difficult journey ahead of me.

The following day, as I started to walk back to my dorm room after finishing one of my college classes, I noticed that my heart felt as though it were beating out of my chest and my arm was turning purple. Several of my friends gathered around me and took my pulse as I rested on the floor. I was in the lobby area, and people coming in and out of the dorm were all commenting in some way. I heard someone whom I didn't really know at the time but who would later become one of my closest friends say, "Dude! Your arm is completely purple!"

I thought, *"Really? Do you think I don't already know that?"*

Uncertain of my next step, I remembered that Dr. Frazier had given me his personal cell-phone number and told me to call him anytime I needed to talk to him. I called him and explained the situation and my symptoms, and he advised me to go to an emergency room as soon as possible. He gave me the location where he wanted me to go and told me that he would contact the doctors to give them advance notice of my arrival and inform them of my condition and what tests had been completed. He said that if I got any worse, I should call 911 and have them transport me by ambulance.

Nathan, a college friend of mine, drove me to the ER. When I arrived, the admittance nurse took my vitals. My heart was beating 180+ beats per minute, and she paged for additional medical staff. Within a minute, I had an entire team of medical personnel rushing toward me. They put me on a transport bed and took me immediately to the triage room.

Everything began to spin out of control. The medical team fired off questions at me.

"Can you tell us your name?"

"David," I responded vaguely.

"David, we need you to take off your shirt quickly, or we're going to have to cut it off."

I followed the medical team's instructions and then was suddenly being hooked up to multiple machines.

"David, you're going to be okay," one of the nurses reassured me as she smiled and squeezed my hand.

Once my heart rate and circulatory condition had improved, doctors started ordering additional tests as I lay there in what seemed like a blurred dream, looking at the bright medical lights above. In a distance, I saw Nathan on the phone with my mother, trying to walk her through what had happened and providing updates as they became available.

Throughout the late evening and the early hours of the next day, doctors continued to monitor and review the tests that had been conducted. The results always came back negative. Nothing could explain what was causing the severe imbalance of my upper thoracic region. The cardiologist assigned to my case conducted a stress test and an echocardiogram. He concluded that I had inappropriate tachycardia, a condition in which the heart rate beats faster than normal,[3] which resulted in the severe palpitations. I was put on additional medication, which they would continue to monitor to help slow my heart rate.

Doctors later advised that it would be best for me to return home immediately. Based on my current condition, they felt that my body would not be able to withstand the ongoing stress of maintaining schoolwork and seeking out medical care given the severe imbalance of my upper thoracic region and the strain it was putting on my body.

As the hospital prepared the discharge papers, I had a million thoughts going through my mind. Why couldn't the doctors find the answers to my condition? What had caused the inappropriate sinus tachycardia? My mind then shifted to school. Only the last week of exams was left of the fall semester. Would the professors understand my situation, or would I have to retake all of the classes?

CHAPTER EIGHT

Clinging to Hope

For you have been my hope, Sovereign LORD, my confidence since my youth. From birth I have relied on you; you brought me forth from my mother's womb. I will ever praise you.

—Psalm 71:5–6 (NIV)

At around 5:30 on Saturday morning, I found myself boarding an airplane to head back home as a result of my medical emergency. The crew was notified of my condition in case I had another episode and required medical attention. The flight attendant made sure that I was all settled in my first-class seat during the preboarding process. I had flown three times since I had moved to Texas, and I somehow got enrolled in a promotional offer that Northwest Airlines was offering and was given Silver Elite status. Looking back, I'm not sure how I even qualified for this premier status, but God knew that those perks would come in handy with my condition and all of the travel that lay ahead.

Since the flight was early on a Saturday morning, I pretty much had the entire first-class cabin to myself. The flight attendant came over to check if I needed anything else. I kindly stated that I was fine but notified her that I had a very tight connection and would have a wheelchair gate host there to greet me once the plane arrived. She was aware of my medical condition, and I knew that she was doing everything she could to accommodate me. Shortly afterwards, she walked up to the captain, and I assumed that she was informing him of our conversation. I will never forget him looking directly back at me. When we made eye contact, he smiled and gave me a wink. I smiled back.

The boarding process continued. Soon everyone was seated, and we backed out of the gate. Before long, we were jetting down the runway.

Once we were airborne, I scooted over to the window seat next to me, which was free, and looked out on the majestic sunrise. I put my earphones on and pushed play. The first song that came on was "O Praise Him."[4] Something about the view I was seeing and the lyrics about angels' song and our loving praise rising up to Christ our King helped me to begin processing the course of the last few days.

A mixture of emotions surfaced as I listened to the music. Physically and mentally, I was completely exhausted. My health condition, my efforts to maintain my schoolwork, and the constant running to and from doctor's appointments had drained every ounce of energy I had. Inside, I felt broken and defeated. The journey that I had begun was being left behind unfinished.

Every time the song concluded, I repeated it. The line "Turn your ear to Heaven" reminded me that God knew everything I was dealing with, more than anyone else to whom I could try to describe it. He knew my frustrations, the discomfort I was feeling, and my uncertainty regarding what the future held. When I heard "O Praise Him," I remembered that God held my future in His hands. I simply needed to trust Him along the way. This song was one of two that would become a rock to me, a constant reminder of who was truly in control of my life.

When I arrived in Memphis for my connecting flight, the flight attendant made an announcement that there was a passenger on the plane with a medical condition who needed to make a very tight connection, and she asked everyone to stay seated while the wheelchair gate host came on board to get me off the plane. Looking back, I can see that this seemingly small gesture was an important reminder that God was present and was using people around me to help me through this journey into the unknown.

Later that afternoon, I arrived in Dayton, Ohio. I was extremely weak. The airport personnel wheeled me out to meet my mom and sister, who were waiting at the baggage claim. When I spotted them, a sense of relief came over me. I was back in the arms of family.

Over the next few days, all I did was lie on the couch and look out the big front window, watching cars come and go down our street. I couldn't help thinking, *"Is this how life is going to be for me now?"* I had always been a go-getter. The busier my schedule was, the more I seemed to enjoy it. Now

I traveled at a snail's pace, unable even to walk into the other room without becoming out of breath from my heart racing. The simplest activities drained what little energy I had. I was battling discouragement every day.

Christmas came and went. It had always been my favorite holiday, but it wasn't the same. I tried to appear cheerful to those around me, but I lacked energy. Deep down, I felt like there wasn't much to celebrate. At times, I wrestled with God. I asked again and again, *"Did You answer my prayers that evening of October 24 just for me to be left on this earth unable to do anything?"*

After a little time passed, I received an email with the subject line: "Do you really want to know?"

The email read:

David,

Everyone is frustrated when things don't make sense. This does, however, make perfect sense to our heavenly Father, who knew this would happen before this day ever came. This will all work out. In the meantime, ask God to reveal to you His purpose for this trial. Search the Scriptures. This is a precious time for you to learn a special bit of God's wisdom that will help you later in life.

When are you returning to Dallas?

LF

Dr. Frazier had no idea about the conversation that I'd had with God less than twenty-four hours prior to receiving his email. His message hit home and resonated with me, reminding me that God had a reason for the trials I was facing.

As I sat there in my room, my mind shifted back to the conversation I had with my mom on the way back from Alex's surgery when I was a senior in high school. I recalled how I had stated that should I ever face any health situations later in life, I wanted to do my best to keep a positive attitude and inspire others.

No more than a year had passed, and here I was, walking through a significant health crisis. I realized that when negative thoughts began to creep into my mind—not only in this current situation I was walking through, but in life in general—I could allow those thoughts to overcome my mindset and dictate my attitude, or I could rise above them and speak the truth, the Word of God, over them. I determined in my mind that despite the difficult season that might be ahead, I was going to do my best to keep pressing forward, to keep a positive attitude, and to speak the Word of God over the lies of the enemy that would try to consume my mind.

Two days after Christmas, my mom and I traveled to a medical-school hospital about an hour away to continue to seek answers regarding my condition. Dr. Frazier had done some research back in Dallas, and he thought that this might be the best location in our area to resume my medical care. When we arrived, I came in through the ER and was assigned to a room. After what seemed like hours, the ER physician came in to do an evaluation. He had me stand up and relax my shoulders and could see that I had winging of the right scapula.

Then a neurologist came in with several medical students to conduct their evaluation as well. They assumed that it was nerve damage and wanted to conduct an EMG. After I told them that this test had already been done in Dallas and showed negative results, they were at a loss as to what was causing all of the upper thoracic symptoms, including the heart issues. Given that I was stable, they released me later that day and recommended that I go to Cleveland Clinic or back to Dallas because I had a very rare case. On the way home, all I did was look out the car window and wonder, *"What are they missing?"*

Over the next few days, I continued to see different doctors in the area to assess my current condition. Many would tell me point-blank that my case was too complex for them. Others said that it was related to bad posture, and some blew me off entirely.

Five Days Later

With no progress being made in my small town, I knew that I wouldn't be able to find answers to my condition there. Over those couple of weeks, I had given my body the rest that it needed, and I reached out to Dr. Frazier for advice. After discussion with him and my parents, I felt that it would be best for me to return to school while continuing to see doctors in the Dallas–Fort Worth area.

In mid-January, about a month from when I had flown home as a result of my medical emergency, I was once again saying goodbye to my family and embarking on a journey into the unknown, this time back to Dallas. My condition was about the same, but I was learning to live with my limitations, at least for now. For example, I knew that while my left shoulder was being carried higher than normal, anytime that I tried to bring it down to a normal position, my arm would turn purple, and my heart rate would spike even higher. I was quickly learning how to react to what my body was telling me. I carried a wristband pulse reader and stayed in tune with different metrics and how I was feeling overall, and I made adjustments by stopping and resting when I needed it or taking additional beta blockers. *I'm not about to give up,* I told myself on the plane ride back to Dallas. *There has to be an answer.*

When I arrived at my dorm room, I felt like I was home. This city, this dorm, and these friends were my new life, at least for this period of time. God had placed me here and given me a task. I was determined that, despite the obstacles I was facing, I would walk across the graduation stage, no matter how long it might take.

My mom contacted the Vice President of the Dallas Christian College prior to my arrival back at school. At this point, pretty much all of the students and professors across the campus were aware of my condition. The professors were informed that I would likely be missing classes to go to various doctor's appointments in the weeks ahead, and they were told to remain flexible with me.

After settling back into Dallas life, I again found myself in Dr. Frazier's office. He had referred me to one of the top neurologists in Dallas at the University of Texas Southwestern to further assess my case. Unfortunately, this neurologist had a four-month waiting list. *"Four months!"* I thought. *"You have to be kidding! I can't keep going on like this!"*

A month passed, and I was in the same position. I eagerly waited for a call from the neurologist's office, hoping that there would be a cancellation so I could get in earlier, but the call never came. It was now the beginning of February, a little over three months since the accident, and it seemed like I hadn't made any progress.

I had a short break in February over Presidents' Day, so I decided to head home for a long weekend. I had decided at the beginning of this journey that I was going to fight for a sense of normalcy where I could. Yes, my condition gave me limitations, but I was alive and was determined to make the best of my life by maintaining a good attitude and being the best son, brother, and friend I could be.

My sister and I had always been close. Being so far away from her and the rest of my family was difficult. My sister loved the game of basketball and was the starting point guard for the Ayersville High School Varsity girls' basketball team. Ever since she started playing basketball as a kid, I made an effort to be at every game, including the games to which we had to travel. However, that changed when I moved off to college and the distance became a factor.

One of her games happened to fall over Presidents' Day weekend, when I had a break in my class schedule, so I made plans to slip up and surprise her. My best friend, Abel, accompanied me on the trip. He was the same person who, a few months earlier, had said, "Dude, your arm is purple," in the dorm lobby. Our personalities could not have been more different. At the time, he was laid-back and outgoing, someone who just went with the flow and didn't take anything seriously. I, on the other hand, was a structured, reserved, by-the-book kind of person. I'm not sure how we hit it off, but our friendship grew, and we helped to balance each other out. With all that I had going on in my life, I needed someone who was a little more free-spirited. My life was more structured than ever during this time, with all of the appointments I had in addition to my class schedule and schoolwork. Abel always kept a good eye on me, helping to carry things since I had so many restrictions with my condition, looking out for me when I went down stairs, and checking my coloring. Looking back, I can say that his help made a significant difference for me.

Abel came up with the idea to make matching shirts that we would wear to my sister's basketball game. The front of each shirt said:

Two San Antonio Spurs Tickets: $120. To FLY 1200 Miles to See the Lady Pilots Win ... PRICELESS.

On the back of the shirts, "Rose" was printed with her number, 23. We had it all mapped out. We purchased our tickets, and we were off to Ohio early in the morning. It was the first time Abel had ever been on an airplane, so I tried to take his mind off everything happening around him. During that flight, I realized that although I was going through a difficult period, there was still a lot for me to be thankful for. Here I was, sitting next to my friend who had never experienced flying before, while I had already been on over fifty flights.

My mom picked us up at the airport when we arrived sometime in the afternoon. My sister, Christina, still didn't have a clue that I was coming home for the weekend until that evening. She came out of the locker room, and there I was! We ran to each other, and I gave her a big hug.

My family, Abel, and I cheered Christina on throughout the evening, and she and her teammates pulled off a win. It filled my heart with joy to know that I was able to be there to support my sister and cheer her on, something that I deeply missed.

On Saturday, my sister, Abel, my brother, his fiancée at the time, and I all went to Fort Wayne to see a Christian concert together. I wasn't fully feeling up to it as I was still in a good amount of discomfort, but I wasn't going to miss out on enjoying quality time with my family.

On Sunday, we went to church and then came home and hung out as a family, watching movies. Abel and I departed on Monday to head back to Dallas. The weekend went quickly, but it helped to boost my spirits and put a little bit of normalcy back into my life.

Over the course of the next few weeks, I decided to start taking research into my own hands. I took every chance I could to read through medical articles on the internet, trying to identify what was causing all of the issues I had. One evening, I stayed on the computer in the library for a couple of hours, googling my symptoms. I clicked on a website link that read, "Winging scapula injury expert." As I read through the website, the article seemed to be describing several of the symptoms that I had. I was so excited that I said out loud, "This is it!"

My friends around me asked, "What's that?"

I pointed to the website. "This is what I have!"

I called the physician's office during one of the breaks in my class schedule the next day. I was able to talk with the nurse, who answered the phone. She asked me several questions regarding my symptoms, when the injury started, and so forth. Then the nurse placed me on hold. When she came back to the phone, she said, "Dr. Nath would like to speak to you."

The neurosurgeon picked up the phone and started asking me additional questions. After his evaluation over the phone, he said, "I believe you have a significant nerve injury to one of your cranial nerves and would like to see you as soon as possible." He told me that he would put the nurse back on the phone to schedule the appointment, and he wanted it within the week. Spring break was only a few days away, so I scheduled an appointment for then since I would have to travel down to Houston to see him. Our conversation gave me hope, and I was excited. I was also a little nervous because I didn't know what lay ahead.

CHAPTER NINE

Diagnoses

Consider it pure joy, my brothers and sisters, whenever you face trials of many kinds, because you know that the testing of your faith produces perseverance.
—James 1:2–3 *(NIV)*

"Boarding all passengers for Delta flight #6503 to Houston Bush Intercontinental," echoed across terminal E at Dallas/Fort Worth International Airport. As I proceeded to board the plane, little did I know that I would be taking this route far too many times to count in the months and years ahead.

Shortly after my arrival in Houston, my mother and I met up. It was a relief to know that we were both there since we had come in from two different locations. By the time we got our rental car, it was starting to turn dark. It was our first time in Houston, so we didn't have a clue where we were going. We pulled out our maps and tried to decipher the various highways and roads to determine how to get to the downtown area because we initially thought that was where the medical district was.

We made it to the downtown area. Then we drove up and down the streets, looking at our maps and trying to figure out how to get to our hotel. We spotted a police officer, so we rolled down our window to ask him for directions. He informed us that the medical district was about fifteen minutes away and not in the downtown area. After two hours of driving around Houston, we finally made it to our hotel room.

On Thursday morning, I sat patiently in the waiting room of Dr. Nath's office. The nurse walked in and called my name, and my mom and I headed back to the examining room. Shortly after, Dr. Nath walked in and introduced himself to both of us. He asked me to take off my shirt, so I did. He began to observe my current condition and noticed how severely my scapula was penetrating out from my rib cage. He then took a series of pictures, asking me to do different gestures, such as shrugging my shoulders and moving my arms out from my side to above my head.

Afterwards, he informed me that he would be sending me over to Dr. Vennix's office to conduct a full EMG of my neck, brachial plexus area, and lower extremities (legs). I would see him later in the day for the results. This exact test was done back in December on my birthday and had shown negative results, but I hoped that somehow, this time, it would show something to explain my injuries.

Over the next few hours, I was in the office of Dr. Vennix, being poked by small needles going in and out of my neck, shoulder, and legs. It was a mild discomfort, more annoying than painful. Dr. Vennix informed me after the test was completed that there was significant nerve damage. Dr. Nath would go over the findings in further detail with me. Dr. Vennix also said, "In regards to the weakness in your lower extremities and your heart issues, I would advise you to consult with Cleveland Clinic as you have a very complex case." I thanked him for his service, and my mother and I headed out.

Later that afternoon, we met back up with Dr. Nath, who shared the test results with us. "Based on the EMG report," he said, "there is a ninety-percent blockage of your spinal accessory nerve, also known as your eleventh cranial nerve. With the little over four months that has already passed since the initial accident, we need to do a surgery within the next one to two months. Otherwise, the injury could result in permanent damage to this nerve." He went on to explain how the cranial nerve runs from the brainstem down the neck and supplies function and support to the trapezius muscle, which supports the scapula. Due to less than ten percent of the nerve signal firing, there was little being transmitted.

My mother and I were trying to process all of the information coming at us. Being the only parent there at the time, my mom tried to think of and ask as many questions as she could, such as what the risks of the surgery were and what the recovery time would be. Dr. Nath thoroughly walked us through the answers to our questions. Then he looked over at me and said, "David, you are very fortunate. Very seldom do I ever see cranial nerves being damaged in car accidents.

Based on the trauma observed, you could very well have been paralyzed from the neck down. You are a walking miracle."

As we left the doctor's office, I felt relieved to get some answers and more grateful than ever before that I was still alive and had function in my hands and legs. I didn't understand why the previous EMG back in December hadn't shown these results, but I knew that God understood.

The following morning, my mother and I headed out of Houston on two separate planes, one bound for Dallas and the other bound for Detroit. Dr. Nath had requested that I return within the next two weeks to see both a neurologist and a cardiologist for additional testing to begin the workup so I could be cleared for the critical surgery.

Two Weeks Later

"Welcome to Houston Bush Intercontinental," echoed across the airplane intercom. I was back for additional consultation and evaluations.

On this particular trip, my dad came along with my mom. They agreed from the beginning that my mom would be present at all tests I might need to undergo in the months ahead, but both would be present for any surgeries. It was good to have my dad there. I knew that my mom needed the support as well. This process was beginning to be a lot on her as a mother.

The first appointment we had was with Dr. Loftus, the neurologist to whom I had been referred. When he came into the room, he excused my parents and conducted an extensive evaluation on me, testing my reflexes, memory, and balance, how I walked, and the feeling in my hands, arms, and legs.

After his thorough exam, he brought my parents back in and stated that he would like to do additional testing on me. Dr. Loftus looked at my parents and said, "Based on my evaluation, your son will never be able to run or ride a bike again with his current weakness in his legs. The additional testing I would like to do in the near future would include a myelogram and additional MRIs to ensure that there isn't any additional structural damage in the lumbar area. In the meantime, I will go ahead and clear him for this surgery, given the fact that we are racing against the clock to correct the nerve."

Our next appointment was with Dr. Karim, a cardiologist in the Houston area to whom Dr. Nath had referred me. I brought all of the files I had from the cardiologist I had seen in Dallas, hospital records regarding the racing heart episodes, medications prescribed to lower my heart rate, and so forth. Dr. Karim ordered an echocardiogram, an EKG, and a Holter monitor test. The Holter monitor, a test that measures and records your heart's activity for a given period, would be conducted over the course of one week, and I was told to wear the device 24/7.

My parents and I started to discuss preparations for my surgery that evening over dinner. My mom had been in touch with Dr. Nath's office earlier in the day. As we were conversing, all I could think of was my sister back home. What was she up to? How was she doing without our parents there? I realized then just how much this journey was beginning to pull us all in a million different directions.

In the morning, I said my goodbyes as my parents headed out on one flight while I was on another. The component of traveling to seek medical care added its complexity to an already challenging process for myself and my family. I lived by a strict schedule. My calendar was consumed with appointments, travel, and classes. Days seemed to fly by as I crammed so much into my day-to-day routine to keep up with my schoolwork. The constant running to and fro helped to distract me from the inner pain of my past.

A week passed, and I found myself once again going through the checkpoint at DFW International Airport, heading back to Houston. This time, I had wires all over my chest and a decent-sized tracking device attached to my belt that was keeping record of every heartbeat and sinus rhythm.

On this particular visit, I had only a follow-up appointment with Dr. Karim, so I convinced my mother that I would be fine to make the trip without her. Upon my arrival, I took a cab from the airport and went directly to the appointment with Dr. Karim, who evaluated all of the results of the Holter monitor test and the stress test I did that day. The conclusion was that I did have inappropriate sinus tachycardia, which I already knew, and a mild case of mitral valve prolapse. Why the inappropriate tachycardia suddenly came up out of the blue after this accident was the question. In the meantime, Dr. Karim increased my beta blocker and cleared me for the surgery with Dr. Nath.

Friday, April 23—Houston Methodist Hospital

A mixture of emotions ran through me as I sat with my family in the pre-surgery registration area of the Methodist hospital. The last six months since the accident had been a whirlwind of juggling schoolwork, running to numerous appointments, and dealing with the frustration of not getting results from the many tests I endured.

Today was a big day for which I had been patiently waiting and praying for some time. I hoped and believed that once the brachial plexus injury was healed through this surgery, just maybe the rest of my body would heal itself, like a chain reaction.

Throughout my childhood, I had never had a surgery, so all of this was new to me. A nurse came out to the waiting room and announced, "David Rose." I got up and walked toward her, and she asked, "All ready?"

At that moment, a part of my heart sank a little. *"Am I ready for this?"* I asked myself.

The nurses got me all prepped and ready to go. Prior to wheeling me back, the anesthesia team came in and asked me a series of questions. Next, a hospital representative came in to walk me through the hospital waivers I would need to sign in order to proceed with the surgery. I was nineteen years old now, legally old enough to sign on my own behalf, and I was making the most difficult decision I had made so far in my life. There were many risks associated with the surgery.

Afterwards, one of the nurses looked directly at my mom and said, "Ma'am, your son is about to go through an extremely critical operation that most surgeons would not attempt, but I have to say that if there's anyone I would trust to do this surgery, it would be Dr. Nath. Your son will be in good hands."

I hugged each of my family members and said, "See you all on the recovery side," trying hard to be strong for everyone else.

As the medical team wheeled me down the well-lit hallway, my family faded into the distance. I was taken back to OR 8. When they wheeled me into the room, I instantly felt chilled to the bone. The medical team asked if I would be able to climb onto the operating bed, which I did. I lay there, face up, with bright lights directly above me. The oxygen mask was put on, and my body was strapped to the table. The anesthesiologist said, "David, I'm going to start giving you some medicine to relax you. Can you start counting backwards, starting with ten?"

CHAPTER TEN

When God Doesn't Make Sense

When doubts filled my mind, your comfort gave me renewed hope and cheer.
—Psalm 94:19 *(NLT)*

When I woke up in recovery, the first thought that came to my mind was to test the movement of my arms and legs to make sure that I was able to move them. Everything worked! A sigh of relief came over me as I lay there in the post-surgery wing.

My sister came and stayed with me until I was taken back to my hospital room. My family later informed me that Dr. Nath was happy with how well the surgery had gone and had told them that we should know in the morning if it had worked to the level we hoped and prayed it would. Scar tissue and blood had wrapped around the nerve, impacting its function. The nerve was freed up in surgery and shocked, and a test was conducted to determine the function of the nerve. Dr. Nath informed my family that the test had yielded positive results.

At around 8 a.m. the next morning, Dr. Nath came into my room. He asked me if I was feeling like I could get out of bed. He wanted to look at my thoracic region to see if it had improved. I got out of bed and stood straight up, facing the other direction so that he could see the back side of my body. The shoulder area (winging of my scapula) had improved significantly, but Dr. Nath was concerned about why my left side was still being carried higher than normal. He looked at my mom and said, "I was hoping this surgery would correct his entire upper thoracic region, but it appears it hasn't. I believe we are going to have to continue to do some more testing." His words kept echoing in my ears. It wasn't exactly the news I had hoped for.

In the afternoon, I was released from the hospital. My family and I stayed in Houston at a local hotel for a few days while I recovered. I had a lot of downtime to stop and reflect, specifically on God's purpose for this trial I was going through. As I prayed and searched the Scriptures, Romans 8:28 (NIV) became my theme verse:

> *And we know that in all things God works for the good of those who love him, who have been called according to his purpose.*

At this time, God gave me a clear response to the question I had asked back in December: *"David, the story of your trials will go on to help many people."* I didn't quite understand the full context, but I knew that God was going to take all of the trials I was facing and somehow use them for His good.

After a few days in Houston, I had my follow-up appointment with Dr. Nath and was given clearance to return to Dallas. I immediately resumed my schoolwork as I continued through the recovery and rehabilitation process. I had only two weeks left of my freshman year to go, and I knew that I needed to finish strong. I juggled numerous physical-therapy appointments while preparing for my final exams over those long few days.

On Friday, May 9, I completed all of my coursework! By God's grace, He had given me the strength to finish the entire year while shuffling all of the different moving pieces and unexpected circumstances that had come up in my short period of time in Dallas.

Return Visit to Houston

Five days after finishing my first year of college, I found myself boarding yet another plane headed down to Houston. My condition was stable, but my body was compensating in so many ways since the accident. I continued to struggle with my health, not knowing when my heart would have a sudden episode like I had back in December and I would have to be rushed to the hospital. Any light activity, such as walking across campus, would leave me completely out of breath even though I was still taking one of the highest levels of beta blockers. My left arm was constantly going in and out of numbness, and if I didn't carry it the right way, it would turn purple. Balance issues were always at the forefront of my mind. When I went down stairs, I was afraid, not knowing if or when my legs would give out underneath me. My body no longer knew what was so-called normal.

I took a 6 a.m. flight out on Friday because I was scheduled to meet with Dr. Loftus that afternoon to review the course of testing that I would be undergoing over the upcoming week. Dr. Nath and Dr. Loftus had been consulting with numerous other specialists in their fields to determine what the priority should be given my rare and complex case. My doctors determined that it would be best to conduct a myelogram of the cervical, thoracic, and lumbar regions as well as a repeat of the MRI for the thoracic and cervical regions and the spine, both with and without contrast.

After the appointment, I knew that I would have a long upcoming week of multiple tests, so my mom and I decided to make the best of the weekend. On Saturday, we drove down to the beach and hung out for a little while. It was good to get out of the hotel room and enjoy some fresh air and the beautiful day. On Sunday, we decided to stay local.

Monday morning arrived, and we were both up early to check in at the preregistration area of the Methodist hospital. Before long, I was being wheeled back to the procedure room. Moments later, I was lying flat, with my stomach against the cold table. I knew what was coming next, and I cringed.

The doctor conducting the test told me that I was going to feel some pressure in my spine but wouldn't feel any pain because local anesthesia had been applied. I tried so hard to take my mind off what was taking place. I knew that any activity could cause damage since there was a needle pushed into my spine. Dye was then injected. Shortly after that, the needle was taken out. Relief filled my mind. The worst of the procedure was over.

A series of different X-rays was taken as I lay there on the procedure table, hoping that the doctors would find something to explain my symptoms. Before I knew it, I was being wheeled into the recovery room. A nurse came to check on me, and my mom joined me before long. Soon I was released.

The next morning, I was back at the hospital. I had an IV started so they could inject the different contrast dye into me, and a series of different MRIs was taken. As I lay there in the enclosed MRI machine, I once again thought back to the conversation I had with my mom on our way home from visiting Alex in the hospital when I was a senior in high school. I knew that God had me on this journey, and I was going to do my best to keep a good attitude.

On Wednesday, I had a follow-up appointment with Dr. Loftus. As we sat down in the examine room, he informed me that, for the most part, all of the tests had come back normal. I had a few discs bulging mildly, but nothing that would result in the symptoms I had.

I was then referred to a movement specialist, adding yet another name to the list of doctors already overseeing my care. He assessed my condition and thought that it would be best to try to relax the left shoulder area by giving me a series of Botox injections. Given that this was not a typical treatment method at the time (though it is more common these days), my mom had to call our health insurance company to get approved since it would be several thousand dollars for the medication alone.

Inwardly, I didn't have peace about this. I started getting anxious about what could happen. The shoulder was being carried higher than normal for a reason. Anytime it was lowered, my arm turned completely purple, and my heart rate increased rapidly and uncontrollably. Given that my mother and I were both scheduled to fly out later that day, with me heading back to Dallas and my mom back to Ohio, I wasn't comfortable about this at all. We had a lengthy conversation in the exam room.

"David, I don't know what to do," my mother said.

Honestly, I didn't know what to do, either. With the pressure of the doctor advising one thing, receiving the call that insurance would approve the treatment, and my mom teetering back and forth, I decided to proceed even though something inside of me knew that it didn't make sense.

Shortly thereafter, the specialist brought in twelve Botox shots, which were inserted into my neck and all down my shoulder area to see if that would help to decrease the spasms. Thankfully, by God's grace, even with all of the injections, the left shoulder area didn't budge. I would later find out that my intuition was right and this was the worst thing that could have been done in my condition.

Before my mother and I headed back to the airport, Dr. Nath requested that I return to Houston to continue with additional testing. Knowing that I would have to wrap up a few things in Dallas and then fly up to Ohio for a short summer break, we decided to return three weeks later.

Summer Mini-Break

In the midst of all that I had going on, I knew that the summer would fly by. The doctors wanted to get as many tests scheduled as they could while I was on summer break. Knowing this, I decided to stay in Dallas instead of moving home for the entire summer.

Thankfully, my roommate's sister, who had two little children at the time and lived in Mesquite on the outskirts of Dallas, took me in. They would essentially become my Dallas adopted family. Anytime that I needed to get my mind off what I was going through, they were right there to pick me up. Looking back, I can see that this family was God-sent. They were a blessing in more ways than they will ever know.

On Wednesday, June 2, I flew home for a couple of days. My brother was getting married on the following Saturday, and I was the best man, so I wanted to make sure that all went well. Extended family drove in from Xenia to the small town of Defiance on Saturday. It was good to see my grandparents, aunt, uncles, and cousins all gathered for this special occasion. I hadn't seen them in over a year because I had been too weak to travel during the Christmas holiday.

My brother's big day arrived, and we couldn't have asked for a more beautiful day. As the bride and groom exchanged their vows, I thanked God not only for the amazing day, but also for keeping me around and giving me the opportunity to witness and take part in my brother's wedding.

It was a small town, so it seemed like everyone knew of the accident and all that I had endured. Throughout the day, people were constantly asking how I was doing, expressing their concern, and providing their opinions. Had I tried seeing fill-in-the-blank doctor? Perhaps it was fill-in-the-blank condition? Everyone had a diagnosis. I would listen politely and then somehow find a way to change the subject.

Deep down, while I was grateful for people asking how I was and showing their interest, I was frustrated about still not having clear answers regarding my condition. Everywhere I turned, I had constant reminders. I saw a glimpse of what my family was facing on a regular basis while I dealt with similar interactions in Dallas with professors, friends, and church members. The words that I found most comforting were from those who said something like, "I'm sorry you are going through this. I'm praying for you." They didn't try to give advice but were straightforward in acknowledging that I was going through something difficult, and they reassured me that they were praying for me.

Over the next few days, I enjoyed hanging out with my family before departing for Dallas on Wednesday. My summer mini-break at home was far too short. I longed to stay and enjoy a normal summer in the presence of family and friends, something I then realized how much I missed.

I'm Done. I'm Finished.

I returned to Dallas for only a couple of days before heading out again. I was working a part-time job to help my parents offset my travel costs, medical bills, and personal expenses. Thankfully, God had blessed me with a job at a large hotel company that enabled me to have discounts on hotel rooms, which I was utilizing frequently with all of my travel.

At 3:35 on Sunday afternoon, I boarded a plane bound for Houston, heading down for additional testing. We pushed back on time and proceeded to the runway, just to find out that Houston Bush Intercontinental had closed their airport due to a thunderstorm that was hitting there. The crew and all of us passengers sat on the runway for an hour until we were informed that we had to go back to the airport to deplane and refuel. We reboarded at 6:15 p.m. and pushed back yet again, only to sit on the runway until 7 p.m., when the pilot informed us that we were not able to take off due to weather still being bad in Houston.

As I sat there in my seat, I thought, *"What am I going to do if this flight gets canceled? Should I consider driving to Houston?"* I was running on little sleep because I worked the overnight shift at the hotel. I was scheduled to have an aortogram, arteriogram, and venogram conducted early the next morning. It would be an invasive series of tests in which dye would be injected into the aorta, blood vessels, and veins to monitor blood flow.[56]

I called my mom once we deplaned yet again. She had

landed just before the storm hit, and she had already picked up the rental car. She informed me that the rain had died down, but the flooding was bad all around the city. It was now shortly after 8:30 p.m. I was exhausted, getting impatient, and asking God what I should do. The burden of dealing with my health, work, and all of the travel, on top of the unpredictability of it all, was weighing heavily on me.

By 9:15 p.m., most of the passengers had already given up and left the airport, but I sat there, still hopeful that the flight would be cleared to leave. Shortly after 9:30 p.m., the gate agent came on the intercom and stated that the air traffic controllers in Houston had cleared the plane to take off. A sigh of relief came over me, and I thanked God as we quickly boarded the plane.

We arrived in Houston around 10:45 p.m., and my mother was outside the airport to pick me up. I hopped into the car, and we proceeded to the hotel, which was located next to the medical district. Exhausted from the long day of travel, we headed straight to bed.

Monday morning came too soon. I was back in the Methodist hospital in the preregistration area at 6 a.m. It seemed like this hospital was becoming all too familiar to me. Moments after I arrived, I heard my name echo across the room. The nurse informed my mom that she would be out once I was all prepped.

Twenty minutes later, when I was all ready to go back to the procedure room, in came my mom to provide some encouragement. I was proud of how strong she was even though I knew this was taking a toll on her.

Then the medical team came in and wheeled me back to the procedure room. A catheter was placed through my groin area, and the dye was inserted. Doctors went through a series of X-rays, taking pictures of veins, arteries, et cetera. Next, they had me sit up and force the shoulder down into place, and they took additional X-rays.

After nearly two hours, the nurse informed me that the procedure was done, and I was taken back into the recovery room. In order to stop the bleeding in the groin area, I was placed in a somewhat large clamp contraption. The device had a flat end that I sat on and a similar circular flat end that was clamped down on my groin area. The clamp was then tightened firmly in order to help clot the blood so the bleeding would stop.

Later that afternoon, I was released from the hospital. A nurse told my mom to keep an eye on me as I could easily bleed out. I thought, *"That's not something you want to tell my mom."* Sure enough, every hour, if not twice an hour, my mom came to check on me.

"Are you doing okay? Has the bleeding stopped?"

Each time, I responded, "I'm fine, mom. I will let you know if I need anything."

The following day, I rested in my hotel room. I had to continue to lie flat without lifting anything until twenty-four hours had passed. That evening, I was feeling up to getting out of the hotel room, so my mom and I headed to a nearby restaurant to eat.

Christina called on our way back to the hotel to see how I was doing. It was always good to hear her voice. I know it was hard on her not being able to be present and know how things were going for me. We conversed for a good while before she got off the phone to finish up her homework.

In the morning, I had a follow-up appointment with the movement specialist. I could tell that his demeanor was off compared to the last time I saw him, less than a month before. He said that there wasn't much more he could do for me.

When we were in the elevator, heading out of the doctor's office, my mom seemed overly quiet, not like her normal self, as I expressed my opinion on the doctor's visit. I looked at her and asked what was wrong, and her response seemed vague. I continued to press her to be upfront and honest. She held back for a moment but eventually told me that the doctor could not find anything that would explain any problems with the blood flow to my left arm from the procedure that I had done on Monday. Knowing that wasn't all from the look on her face, I pressed her for more.

"David, one of the doctors thinks that it could be psychological. They want to have one additional doctor, a vascular surgeon, review the test results prior to sending you to a psychiatrist."

I threw up my hands, looked at my mom, and said, "I'm done, mom! How I could make my arm completely turn purple is beyond me. I'm so tired of all the procedures and not getting answers! I will just learn to live with my disabilities as I have done since the accident."

Back in the hotel room, I wrestled with God in my thoughts. I was so disappointed and frustrated with this entire process and my complicated past. Since the accident, I had been through so much, yet I had so little to show for it. What were the doctors missing? Why couldn't I just go and get the answers I needed and be done with all of this?

That evening, I made a declaration to God:

Father, I will go and see one additional doctor, the vascular surgeon to which they referred me today. I will make a promise to You that if You would help this doctor to find an answer to my circulatory problems, I will continue on this journey of seeking medical care, and I will devote my future life to serving You in whatever capacity You lead me.

Peace came over me as I laid my head down to sleep after a long and tiresome day.

CHAPTER ELEVEN

A Miracle

Everything is possible for one who believes.
—Mark 9:23 *(NIV)*

As I sat in the office of Dr. Shah, a vascular surgeon, I didn't know what to expect. Would this be another doctor who stated that my case was too complicated? Would he be like the last doctor I had seen, who thought that it was all in my head? On the surface, I pretended that I had blown off what the last doctor had shared with my mom, but it was bothering me. I felt hurt, alone, and somewhat like an outcast. These feelings built on top of the inner pain that I was still coping with from my childhood experiences.

Everywhere I turned, someone was always asking me how I was doing. My short response was: "I'm doing good. How about yourself?" Deep down, I wasn't fully fine, but I didn't really know how to express myself.

I didn't understand why I couldn't just show up and the

doctors would find what was wrong and correct the problem so I could move on with my life. Every time reports came back normal, it made me doubt myself and question this journey even more. I suppressed my feelings, inwardly becoming increasingly frustrated and confused.

There were moments when I would bounce around in my mind the possibility that there was something I was doing that brought on the symptoms. Each time I considered this, I would come to the conclusion that the symptoms were real and had all started after the accident. Deep down, I knew that something was seriously wrong despite what others might say or think.

In the examining room, Dr. Shah did an extensive review of my left brachial plexus area. He then asked me to try to bring my left shoulder down to a normal position, and he noticed right off that my arm turned purple. While I held it there, he took my pulse in my left arm. He then said, "David, go ahead and allow your arm to go back to a comfortable position." Once I did so, he said, "Can you bring it back down for me?" and I did.

"David, there is no pulse in your arm when you bring your arm down, and when you allow it to go back to a comfortable position, the pulse returns. There is definitely something going on."

He looked at his charts to see if the test results of Monday's aortogram, arteriogram, and venogram had come through.

"David, it appears that we haven't received the scans yet. I will have my nurse follow up, and I will give you a call on your cell phone later today with my interpretation of the reports."

I simply thanked him, and so did my mom. Then we left the doctor's office.

My heart doctor, Dr. Karim, had additional testing already lined up for me in the afternoon that was scheduled as part of this visit to Houston. I had another EKG, an echocardiogram, and a twenty-four-hour Holter monitor put on to see if my heart condition had gotten any worse since my initial testing in April.

Afterwards, my mom and I grabbed dinner. On our way back to the hotel, I looked down at my watch and saw that it was already 7:30 p.m. I thought, *Well, it appears that Dr. Shah is not going to call me back.* Just as I was thinking that, I had an unknown phone number come up on my cell-phone screen, and I answered.

"David, this is Dr. Shah. I wanted to let you know that I reviewed your test results from Monday's procedure. There is an interference that is impacting blood flow to your arm. I would like you to come into the office tomorrow to discuss next steps. I will have my nurse call you in the morning to schedule a time."

I thanked him and told him, "Have a great evening. I appreciate you calling!"

I was happy to hear that Dr. Shah had found something. I recapped what he had said to my mom as we continued our way back to the hotel.

The next morning, Dr. Shah's nurse called and asked if 10 a.m. would work to meet with the doctor. I didn't have anything else scheduled on that Wednesday except a follow-up with Dr. Nath in the afternoon, so I said that would work fine.

As I sat in the waiting room yet again, a mixture of emotions was surfacing. I was excited at the chance to find answers but, at the same time, nervous about what our next steps might be.

Dr. Shah's nurse called my name, and my mother and I walked back to one of the examining rooms. Dr. Shah came in shortly after, sat down, and looked both of us in the eye.

"After reviewing the test results and examining your arm, I see that there is an obstruction that is preventing the blood flow from getting throughout your left arm. This is called thoracic outlet syndrome. It is a rare disorder that occurs when the blood vessels are compressed between your collarbone and first rib. This disorder can occur after physical trauma, which in your case was the car accident. Likely, with the seat belt coming across your left shoulder area, the rib cage shifted, causing the first rib and the collarbone to be compressed, which is limiting the blood flow to your arm. Your brain is ultimately holding your shoulder higher without you knowing it to prevent it from losing circulation altogether."[7]

My mind shifted off for a split second as my mom went on to ask him a few questions.

"My brain is holding the shoulder up in place," I said to myself.

I picked back up with the conversation when Dr. Shah said, "David, I would like to refer you to the doctor who wrote the book on this syndrome."

My mom and I looked at each other for a split second and then looked back at the doctor. "Where might that be?" we asked.

"Dr. Harold Urschel at the Baylor Hospital in Dallas," Dr. Shah replied.

A sigh of relief washed through me. At least this doctor was back where I lived, in Dallas.

Later that evening, I thanked God for an answer to my prayer. He had me on this journey, and I knew that I needed to be the light to the world around me in whatever capacity I could despite the obstacles I might face. I held to the promise I had made Him and would wait for His direction regarding how and when He wanted to use me.

On the final day of this visit to Houston, I had back-to-back appointments scheduled. My cardiologist evaluated the Holter monitor, EKG, and echocardiogram results and concluded that my condition had stayed about the same. The rapid heart rate with any light activity, such as walking across campus, was still very much relevant in the reports. The cardiologist upped my beta-blocker medicine and stated that he wanted to keep an eye on this.

Afterwards, I met with Dr. Loftus, my neurologist, and he increased my muscle relaxer even more to help decrease the tightness and spasms occurring in my legs. He was a doctor whom I would continue having to see on a regular basis.

Later that evening, my mom and I said our goodbyes for now at the airport. I hugged her before we departed on separate flights.

One Step Closer

Less than two weeks after I met with Dr. Shah and received the referral to Dr. Urschel, I found myself sitting in the waiting room at Baylor Hospital. On my journey so far, I had spent so much of my time just waiting—waiting in hospital rooms, waiting in doctor's offices, and most importantly, waiting for answers. Would today be the day for additional clarification?

With this appointment being right there in Dallas, I convinced my mom that she didn't need to fly down to be with me. The cost associated with the back and forth to the numerous appointments had been piling up, and I wanted to help cut costs where I could even though I knew that my mom wanted to be there.

Shortly after my arrival, Dr. Urschel, a cardiothoracic surgeon, walked into the exam room. He introduced himself and stated that he had reviewed my case notes from Dr. Shah and my test results. Then he examined me thoroughly. Afterwards, he explained the next steps he wanted to take, which included additional testing that would need to be done before he could recommend a course of treatment.

Within the week, I had a series of EMG tests, blood work, and additional scans completed prior to meeting back with Dr. Urschel.

"David," he said, "test results confirm that you have thoracic outlet syndrome." He went on to explain in further detail what that meant.

During our conversation, I informed him that I had

received a series of Botox injections into my neck to see if that would relax the area.

Clearly frustrated, he said, "That was the worst thing they could have done for you at the time. If the shoulder had dropped as they intended and hoped it would, the subclavian artery would have been cut off, essentially preventing blood flow to your arm. Likely, within an hour or less, you would have had permanent damage, resulting in your arm having to be amputated.

"Based on your current condition, I recommend surgery. We need to go in and free up space to allow more room through the thoracic outlet area for your veins, artery, and nerves. The procedure entails removing your first rib and possibly your second rib, but we'll know more once we are in surgery."

I nodded and asked a series of questions regarding recovery time and risks associated with the surgery before agreeing to move forward.

Given my ongoing treatment, Dr. Urschel requested that I receive clearance from my cardiologist and neurologist to have the surgery, which meant another trip back to Houston.

That evening, I was so grateful that I was finally receiving answers. It seemed like things were coming together slowly but surely at this point, nine months after the accident.

Over the next two weeks, I flew down to Houston for testing and clearance for surgery, started registering for fall classes, and moved back into the dorms, all while making the last-minute preparations for my surgery.

On Friday evening, I managed to squeeze in some time

with my friends, and we all hung out and went out to dinner together. I cherished these times of simply hanging out and being silly college students, moments that I rarely got to experience. On our way back to the dorm, I heard "When I Think About the Lord" by Shane & Shane[8] on one of the local Christian stations. The song spoke so clearly to me. When we made it back to the dorm room, I asked my friends the name of the song we had just heard, and I googled it later.

The next morning, I was up and about early. I went to the Christian bookstore to pick up the CD because I just had to have that song. It was amazing to see how God put little things in my path that kept me encouraged and pressing forward. I put the CD in my car and began listening to it on my way back to the college. Every time the song concluded, I hit the back arrow of my CD player to listen to it again. The upbeat lyrics were perfect, and this song became one of my top favorites to listen to over and over.

On Monday, August 16, my family flew in. It was tradition for us to grab a dinner of my choice the night before my surgery since they knew I would not be up to eating for a while.

Tuesday morning came all too quickly. By this time, I knew the drill. I could have no food or drinks after midnight. I needed to wear loose clothing and arrive early. I was familiar with the registration process and surgery prep. Oh, and how could I forget the hospital representative who would come in with pages of forms and waivers I would need to sign? She walked me through the risks associated with the surgery, which, let me add, included death. Once again, at the age of

19, I was signing a release form and making this huge decision on my own. In addition to the waivers, given the risk of this surgery, I had to sign my approval to be given a blood transfusion if I should need it, so I did.

After I signed the forms, my family started giving me their hugs and encouraging words, and they spoke prayers over me.

I was taken back to the pre-surgery wing of Baylor Hospital, and my mom was able to accompany me there. I had one of my earbuds in my ear, and I continued to listen to music. Dr. Urschel had one of the neurosurgeons on staff come in and evaluate me to get his opinion as well, which neither my mother nor I was expecting. When he felt the back of my neck, he noticed right off that I had a bulge near the brainstem on my left side, something that I had notified the doctors of a couple of days before the surgery. I assumed that it was from all of the tension I had in my neck from the imbalance of my shoulders, which put a lot of strain on my neck and lower back area.

The neurosurgeon and my cardiothoracic surgeon went out into the hallway and had a heated conversation regarding my case. I couldn't quite pick up the entire conversation, but I knew that they had a difference of opinion. The neurosurgeon thought that there was something else going on that needed to be resolved before taking me into surgery to remove the rib(s).

As I lay there, I had so much going through my mind. It seemed like everyone I saw had his own opinion. I looked over at my mother and thought about how much I hated putting her through all of this. I was struggling on my end, but I couldn't begin to imagine what she was thinking as a mother. Here was her son, going through one thing after another. I was facing a major surgery, and now doctors were having a very heated conversation outside, but there was nothing she could do to take any of it away. I thought about how much that had to hurt her.

In that moment, I clung to that Shane & Shane song, where the lyrics speak of the Lord healing us "to the uttermost."[9] I began to declare that softly and imagined Him picking me up, turning me around, and setting my feet on solid ground.

Moments later, Dr. Urschel came back into the room and motioned for the medical team to take me to surgery. He was stubborn but was confident that he was making the right decision, something that I liked about him.

My hand slipped out of my mother's palm as I was wheeled down the well-lit hallway.

I climbed onto the operating table, and the team began their preparations. The oxygen mask came on, and anesthesia medicine was placed into my IV. As I started counting backwards, I prayed, "God, keep me safe."

Several hours later, I woke up in the recovery room. This time, I had tubes coming out of my body, and the discomfort was more intense.

My mom came around the curtain shortly thereafter and extended her arm to me. "David, the doctor said you came through quite the trooper. Everything went really well from a procedure standpoint."

"Good news," I thought as I drifted back to sleep.

My recovery time in the hospital was much longer this time. Over the next few days, nurses came in frequently to change out my bandages, monitor the chest-tube drainage, check my wounds, and so forth. The resident who had been training under Dr. Urschel for the last five years came in one to two times each day as well to conduct her normal checkups on me. During one of those rounds, she informed me that my case was the worst they had seen. Internally, my thoracic region had severe swelling and an extreme number of muscle spasms occurring. The first rib and collarbone were practically touching each other. "David," she said, "you are very fortunate that you didn't lose your arm, as the blood flow going to your arm was very minimal."

Once again, even though the process continued to take longer than I initially wanted, God had brought the right doctors at the right time and kept me from further harm.

I continued to progress nicely in the days ahead and was released in less than a week. My family and I stayed at a nearby hotel for a few days prior to us all heading back home to Ohio for me to recover.

Three weeks after the surgery, I was back at the doctor's office for a follow-up appointment. Dr. Urschel told me that everything looked good and the shoulder would take a little time to come down due to the post-surgery swelling. And so it did. A little over a month and a half after the surgery, my thoracic and shoulder areas were even with each other. Deep down, I hadn't been sure that I would ever see that again. I knew that God had performed a series of miracles, and I was grateful.

CHAPTER TWELVE

Unlocking the Lower Compartment

Confess your trespasses to one another, and pray for one another, that you may be healed.
—James 5:16 *(NKJV)*

Two Months Post-Surgery

Over the last few months, we had made progress toward finding answers to what was causing my various symptoms. At this point, I was down to two major complaints: my heart racing uncontrollably with any activity and the spasms constantly occurring in my legs. Both of these symptoms kept me from doing most activities. I often found myself sitting on the sidelines, just watching instead of participating. I longed to be normal and to enjoy college activities, such as playing basketball with my friends, running, or simply walking across the campus without being out of breath.

Determined to continue seeking answers, I pressed forward, believing that I would receive an explanation for what was causing my symptoms. While I was home for a few days in October over my fall break, my parents scheduled me to see a respected local neurosurgeon in the Fort Wayne area. During the consultation, he advised that my case was very complicated and over his head. I appreciated him being upfront and honest instead of wasting more time running unnecessary tests. He advised me to follow up with the Cleveland Clinic hospital. When he mentioned that, I recalled how Dr. Vennix had told us the same thing back in March.

My mom and I thanked him as we exited the doctor's office. I spent the next two days of my short break enjoying time with family before heading back to Dallas. One thing this experience had taught me was just how precious every day was, and I was soaking up every minute that I had with my supportive, loving family.

A few weeks passed, and I found myself sitting once again in terminal E at the Dallas/Fort Worth airport, my thoughts drifting in a hundred different directions as I waited for the airplane to arrive. I dreaded the thought of traveling to another city for more testing and consultation though I wanted to find additional answers to my condition.

It was hard to believe that a year had already passed since the accident. I had become quite the frequent flyer and had been on over seventy different flights, traveling to one location after another, since the accident. I often felt like I was running to and fro while desperately trying to catch my inner breath.

"Now boarding all passengers for Cleveland, Ohio, through gate E6," an airline representative announced over the intercom. I began gathering my belongings, and as I boarded the plane, I said to myself, *"The journey to a new destination on the travel map of recovery is beginning."*

When I arrived in Cleveland, my mother met me at the airport, stronger and more supportive than ever. Our journey seemed like it would never end, and every aspect of it took a toll on us all. Yes, I was the person enduring the medical aspect, but my family sacrificed just as much along the way. I was prouder and more grateful than ever before, and I thought, *"How can I put anything else on them? The past is the past. Why bring it out into the open?"* My schedule had been consumed with travel, schoolwork, and treatments, but the past was catching up to me. Daily I felt like I had to put on a fake smile while inwardly struggling with my distress. I had lost countless hours of sleep, lying and tossing on numerous nights, as I rehashed my past in my mind.

Thursday morning came quickly. When I awoke, I felt a bit of eagerness to find answers, but at the same time, I dreaded the thought of seeing another doctor. I had lost count of the number of specialists I had seen over the last year, many of whom would review my case and instantly say, "I haven't seen anything like this since med school," or, "This is an extensive case. Let me refer you to the following specialist." I found it difficult to quarterback all that was coming at me. Each time I stepped into a doctor's office, I would cringe inside. The thought of having to go through all of my medical history again, doctors I had seen, tests, surgeries, and so forth made me feel like a broken record. I was getting tired of excuses. I just wanted answers so I could get on with my life.

"David Rose," I heard the nurse call out as I sat in the doctor's office. My mother and I proceeded back to yet another exam room. Fifteen minutes passed, and in walked a pain-management doctor. This didn't seem like a specialist I needed to see, but deep down I knew that we were taking a step in the right direction. The doctor reviewed my files and examined my body extensively. Then he told me that he was referring me to a cardiologist for additional workup there at Cleveland Clinic.

At the scheduling desk, the receptionist said that the soonest she could get me in would be the following week on November 23 and 24. I looked at my mother and said, "Good thing I purchased an airline ticket for a span of two weeks."

On our drive into our hometown of Defiance, Ohio, I noticed that things hadn't changed too much since I had moved to Dallas a little over a year ago. Defiance was no doubt a night-and-day difference from the city in which I was now used to living. It sure was a nice change to come home to the comfort of family and friends and the peacefulness of the town.

Before I knew it, the weekend flew by, and my mother and I were headed back to Cleveland for the consultation with the cardiologist. Afterwards, I wrote the following in my journal:

November 24, 2004: I don't understand the complexity of this journey. It seems like it will never end. The last two days have been consumed with my body being poked and probed, records being reviewed, and additional testing being requested.

I will be heading back to Dallas tomorrow morning to wrap up the next couple of weeks of this semester. Doctors informed me today that extensive additional testing will need to be done on my heart and autonomic nervous system to determine the cause of the unexplained rapid heart rate and light-headedness. The test will require me to travel back to Cleveland for a full autonomic cardiovascular panel that takes a full day of testing, with additional consultation with the cardiology department, which is scheduled for Monday, December 20.

When I arrived back in Texas, I felt as though I were swimming in a troubled sea, constantly struggling for a breath of fresh air. The more I pretended that my life was okay, the more waves came barreling against me, crushing, crushing, crushing me!

Life was hitting me from every angle. There was the pressure of college studies, my health problems, constant travel, worry, financial obligations, and work. I felt like I was a ship about to sink at any moment. The waves just kept coming. As the water began to seep in, the storage that was already onboard became heavier and heavier. I had remained so strong throughout this journey for everyone around me, but my hidden past kept stealing my joy.

The challenges related to my health, the impairments and limitations, all continued to build on top of my past. The past that I had tried so desperately to cover up and forget about was becoming too heavy for the structure of the ship to support. As the captain, I felt an uneasy feeling in the pit of my stomach, knowing that I needed to take action in order to survive. The baggage that I had stored deep, deep down in the lower compartment needed to be brought out and thrown overboard, or else I would face more challenging times ahead.

"But how?" I asked myself. *"How?"*

The lower compartment was a location that I feared, resented, and ultimately avoided due to the painfulness of the emotions that were packed tightly in there. I wished that it were as simple as throwing the dead weight overboard.

The world around me viewed me as a courageous, faithful, spirited young man who, despite all odds, continued to trust in the Lord in uncertain times. Little did my family members, friends, professors, and co-workers know that my inner distress was crippling me.

People saw me as independent and confident, and I thought that if I were to reach out to someone for help, people would view me as incompetent or less of a man. The guilt, shame, and frustration were hampering my ability to become the God-driven young man that He had created me to be.

In public, I felt like an actor who always had to put on the mask, the fake smile, pretending that all was well even though the inner walls were crumbling piece by piece. I had learned this skill at a very young age, being a pastor's kid. The dual life of being one person in the spotlight and another one when the curtain went down was stripping my physical energy and draining the life from me.

At a point of desperation, I prayed for direction regarding how to begin the process of unlocking the lower compartment where I stored the mixed emotions that were hampering my ability to move forward. The following scripture came to mind:

Confess your trespasses to one another, and pray for one another, that you may be healed.
— ***James 5:16*** *(NKJV)*

I was prepared at that moment to begin the journey of healing. I didn't know the course, but I couldn't keep going on like this. I prayed about which of my friends in Dallas whom I trusted and had built a rapport with would be the right person for me to confide in. I needed someone to help me through the process. It was a difficult decision but ultimately a step that was required in order for me to move forward.

Like second nature, a young man whom I trusted and respected and who was biblically sound popped into my mind. Picking up the phone and taking the first step in the right direction was dreadful. Reluctantly, I dialed his number while debating in my mind whether I should quickly hang up the phone.

He answered, and I struggled with words. I managed to say, "Hey, man, I have something that I really need to get off my chest. Are you available to come over?"

Without hesitation, he said that he would be right over. I dropped to my knees and prayed for the strength and ability to open the lower compartment.

Twenty minutes later, I heard a knock at the door. I was still debating whether I should make up something that sounded urgent instead of telling him what I really needed to get off my chest. Wrestling with the enemy, I reminded myself what I had set out to do: seek healing and release the past.

I invited him in, and he took a seat. We started talking, mainly small talk. A bit of awkwardness hung in the air, and I told him, "The reason I have called you over here is that I need to get something off my chest." Silence filled the room as I paused for a moment.

"As a very young child, I was abused sexually by an older gentleman. The abuse was very intense and went on for years." My voice caught as I started getting choked up. "Daily I felt the guilt, shame, and disgrace suffocating me. I have struggled each day, gasping for air."

Relief filled my inner soul. I felt that I no longer carried this burden alone. Then I thought, *"Will he think of me differently? Will he judge me? Will he treat me like an outcast?"* Dead silence filled the room as I waited for his response.

"David," he said. "I can't begin to place myself in your shoes, but the first thing that you have to accept is this is not your fault. Today, you took the first step of moving forward." He looked directly into my eyes and told me that he would pray for me, and he encouraged me to pray for what direction to take.

"David, I'm here for you in any way that I can be," he said.

A little later, he left, and I breathed a sigh of relief. I had taken the first step, and it was a major breakthrough in my life. I no longer carried this burden alone. A friend now knew what I was dealing with in addition to all of my current struggles that had piled on top of my past.

As I sat there quietly, alone in my living room, I realized that the physical injuries I had endured following the accident were visible to the eye, but my inner emotional distress had gone unnoticed by the world around me. Each of these would require its own healing process.

CHAPTER THIRTEEN

The Rose Household

Blessed be the God and Father of our Lord Jesus Christ, the Father of mercies and God of all comfort, who comforts us in all our tribulation, that we may be able to comfort those who are in any trouble, with the comfort with which we ourselves are comforted by God.

—2 Corinthians 1:3–4 *(NKJV)*

When I was growing up, it seemed that there was not a dull moment in the life of the Rose family. We, like many other families, had to juggle the scheduling of different extracurricular activities in which my siblings and I were involved. My parents allowed each of us to choose only one sport to participate in throughout a given school year. Once we committed to a given sport, my parents would require us to see the season to completion. My parents wanted to instill in us at an early age that once we gave our word to something, we would give it our absolute best and see it through to the end. Once the school year was up, we could switch sports.

Even from a young age, I was never a huge sports fan. I

tried out for cross country one year and about died running the eight miles that we often had to run during practice. Let's just say that the end of the season couldn't come soon enough for me. I gave it only one year and then switched to track. I found the shorter distance much more suitable for me, but even so, I only ran track through my junior-high years.

In addition, we were required to participate in either band or choir, or we could choose to do both, through our junior-high years. Once we got into high school, we had the option of continuing with it or dropping it. I participated in both choir and band for most of my junior-high and high-school years. I found the performing arts to be a better fit for me than sports. Outside of extracurricular activities and sports, I enjoyed horses. My grandparents owned a horse farm just outside of Dayton in a small town called Xenia, Ohio. I got my love of horses from my mother and my grandpa. In fact, that farm was where my parents met. My mom boarded her horse there.

As I progressed in school, I found some of my escape through horseback riding. Something about being out on a horse and riding through the pasture with the wind blowing helped to soothe me and allowed me an escape from what I was dealing with internally. We were a good three hours away from my grandparents' farm, so I didn't get to ride as much as I wanted to. However, my parents allowed me to start taking horseback-riding lessons in our town of Defiance, and this soon became my new passion.

In the Rose household, we learned at a very young age how to work hard. My parents started a lawn-mowing business when I was seven years old, and it continued to grow in size. On average we, as a family, had about thirty-five to fifty lawns to mow each week, including small residential properties, area churches, businesses, and large corporations, such as Kmart. Our summers were often consumed with the business. In the spring and fall, our schedules intensified as my siblings and I juggled school, homework, and sports practices and competitions while also helping with the business in the evenings.

After school each day, my dad would pick us up, and we would come home and change. Then we hooked up the trailer, and off we went to mow lawns. We had a pretty good routine and kept the mowing to certain nights of the week, typically Monday, Tuesday, Thursday, and sometimes early on Saturday if we were behind because of weather or some type of mechanical problem, such as waiting on a part for a mower. Wednesday night was reserved for church, and Friday evenings and weekends were set aside for family time or doing something in the church. My siblings and I always looked forward to the winter because that meant a season of comparative calmness and rest in our busy lives.

My parents both worked full-time jobs while still juggling the mowing business and raising us kids. The business ultimately kept our family afloat financially. I wouldn't say that we were poor, but money was a topic that came up frequently between my parents. The mowing business had a dual purpose: providing supplemental financial support along with teaching me and my siblings some important lessons. My parents paid us kids a portion of the profits for the work we did, teaching us from a young age how to manage money and how hard work can lead to rewards while also instilling in us a strong work ethic.

The mowing business had another big perk. A certain amount of the income was set aside for our yearly family vacation. I got my love of travel the first time my family boarded a plane and headed back to Texas. We had lived there for a short period of time when I was a child. My father was attending Southwestern Baptist Theological Seminary before taking his first pastoral job, which moved us to South Dakota and, several years later, back to Ohio. As we toured the great state of Texas on our family vacation, it was nice to reminisce about memories we had made there. Throughout my childhood, my family had the privilege of seeing so much of the beautiful land of America, visiting major cities and historical monuments.

My dad held a bi-vocational pastoral role at a local church through most of my childhood, up until my high-school years. On Wednesday evenings and Sundays, my family was in church. I would often find my dad staying up in the wee hours of the morning, preparing for a message. He always did his best to treat family time as a priority even though that meant longer days for him. Pastoring a church came with other responsibilities as well, such as visiting people in the hospital and counseling those walking through a difficult season.

Looking back, I can see that juggling so many different activities and responsibilities at a young age ultimately prepared me for the season I was walking through after the accident and made me better able to maneuver through all that was coming at me. However, on the flip side, the busyness also had a price. The constant "go, go" mentality helped to drown out and silence the inner pain, but that meant the pain was not being dealt with, only pushed deeper and deeper inside me.

When I was growing up in a small town in Ohio, a person's last name was a source of status. If mulitple generations of a person's family had lived in the area, that individual had privileges that an outsider did not. Such people were well known in the town, and they would typically be the starters on the various sports teams, even if they were not the most talented or qualified kids on the team. The children of these established families were the least likely to be bullied in school.

After my family moved to Ayersville, a district in Defiance County, I learned quickly that I was somewhat of an outsider. I didn't have an established family name as so many of my classmates did. My family had bounced around a lot to different school districts before we landed in Ayersville, and I was behind in English and speech. I remember to this day how my second-grade teacher would have us all sit on the floor in a big circle around a flip chart. She would call upon each of us in turn, and we would have to pronounce various words that were inscribed on the chart. I dreaded every time my name was called on. I felt humiliated in front of the class because I often didn't know how to pronounce the words. Instead of the teacher helping me when she saw me struggling, she would instead just sit there and allow silence to fill the room. That particular teacher wasn't the most understanding, to say the very least, and my confidence in myself started to diminish.

I was shy and trying hard to find my place. I found the entire experience of a new school very intimidating. I wanted to make friends but struggled to do so. Toward the middle of the school year, one of my classmates invited me over to his house to stay the night. I tried hard to remain cool, but inwardly I was excited and hopeful to make a friend. In the months ahead, I often went over on Friday nights to stay overnight. Late one evening while I was staying over at this classmate's house, his dad began to touch me inappropriately. I honestly didn't know what was beginning to take place.

In the months ahead, the invitations over to my friend's house came more frequently. For the longest time, I honestly thought that the sexual experiences I was having with his dad were something that every child went through but no one talked about. I assumed that it was preparing me for adulthood. As a young child, I didn't know that what was taking place was wrong, nor did I realize how greatly it would impact my life in the years to come, even well into adulthood.

In school, I continued to try to find my place. Then the verbal bullying started. The names spoken over me rocked me to the core. The words were harsh and demeaning and made me feel belittled. I wanted to escape and to forget all of the anguish building up inside of me.

As time progressed, I continued to have hopes that junior high would be better, but the verbal bullying only intensified. Junior high gave opportunities for people not only in my class, but also in the class above me, to speak unkind, belittling words to me as we passed in the hallways between classes. Each occurrence compounded the frustration and insecurities building up inside of me. I longed to fit in and be normal and accepted, but instead I was becoming less confident in who I was.

In the hallways, anytime I saw someone walking toward me who often spoke harsh, unkind words, I would cringe inside, dreading the unbearable encounter that would soon take place. I would often stop dead in my tracks, turn around, and walk another way, pretending that I had forgotten something in my locker in order to get out of that person's line of sight and hopefully avoid the dreaded interaction. At other times, I would take a longer route to class, which might mean going completely out of my way and taking the stairs down and back up another way even though my next class was still on that same floor.

I had a few friends but never the type of friendship that I truly wanted. Deep down, I longed for a friend to share dreams with, to be a silly kid and do stupid things with. I wanted a friendship that would grow deep roots as we supported each other through thick and thin. I now realize, looking back, that I withdrew from some of the friendships that could have been even more special. It wasn't that I didn't want them. I just couldn't bear to be hurt by anyone else, so I distanced myself. As I buried my pain, I began to compartmentalize it. I started to put up more and more walls to protect what little of myself I felt I had left.

During my junior-high years, I began to piece together

that what was taking place, what my friend's father was doing to me, was not normal. (I later found out that it would be termed "sexual abuse.") Suddenly, I began to feel an immense amount of shame, and a sense of guilt captivated my mind. I thought that maybe I had done something to bring on the abuse.

Being a pastor's kid seemed to come with a whole other level of classification. PKs, in my mind, were supposed to be the ones who had it all together, set the example, stood for what was right, and turned the other cheek when harmed. This pressure built on top of everything else, and I quickly mastered the art of putting on a mask and pretending that all was well while, beneath the surface, my inner life was collapsing.

My dad pastored a small local church. He had the vision to see it grow, and the close-knit families that created the church said that they wanted to be part of seeing the church do great things in the lives of people in the community. However, I would still, to this day, question what their motives and thoughts truly were. The nitpicking that went on in that church just added one more thing on top of my day-to-day struggles.

My relationship with my heavenly Father had a period of doubt. I loved Him, and I believed that He had created me and had plans for my life, but on the flip side, I couldn't understand and fully grasp the reason for all of the emotional pain I was experiencing. I prayed and pleaded. I circled my circumstances in continual prayer, but for whatever reason, my prayers went unanswered. I couldn't understand why bad things happened to good people or why every job for which my parents applied to better our family financially ended up not working out even though we, as a family, had circled it in prayer and believed that it would work out. I felt resentment toward God for a season but chose to continue leaning into Him rather than pushing Him away.

The abuse only seemed to intensify over time. I felt imprisoned, not knowing where to turn. I didn't know what others would think of me if I came out and said what happened. Would it put shame on my dad's church or, for that matter, my family? These questions often bounced around in my mind.

My abuser had told me not to say anything about what was taking place. He was a public figure, well liked in the community, and held several positions. I always thought that it would come down to my word against his, so I remained silent.

My rock through all of the emotional pain was my family. Every evening, I knew that I was at least coming home to a family that loved me, believed in me, and prayed for me. My home and family were the safety net that I needed, a place and a group of people that gave me the chance to put my guard down. Along the way, I told my parents to a certain degree that I disliked the school I was attending, but they never really knew the extent of what I was facing on a regular basis, nor did they know anything about the abuse. Still, to this day, I don't know why I couldn't express my inner pain to them; I just couldn't. I wanted to be strong, didn't want to put anything else on them, and wasn't comfortable with admitting that I wasn't accepted by others. I believe that is what every child truly longs for: to be loved, valued, and accepted.

Inwardly, I was numb. I began silently pulling back, withdrawing from other people to a certain degree. I became more and more insecure with myself. My mind was constantly evaluating the way I looked, my posture, the way I portrayed myself, and the words I spoke. I tried so hard to fit in. I often felt secluded and alone, like a fugitive, trapped in my own world of inner chaos. I read some of the statistics of sexual abuse online, but I didn't know of anyone in my circle who had endured this horrible experience and could relate to what I was experiencing. If any of them had been through it, they, too, were silent. So often, I wondered whether God could still use my inwardly broken life.

I began to focus on the things that I thought I could somewhat control, which included academics and work. I continued to silence the inner pain by staying busy even though I had constant reminders around me of the pain I had endured. I was so ready to graduate and move on with my life, hopeful that my future looked brighter.

Because of what I endured as a child, I began to have the desire to help others, to comfort and encourage them whenever I could. I often found myself speaking encouragement to those who needed it. I would seek out and engage with kids on the playground or in my classes who were alone, bullied, or treated as outcasts. For example, in high school, we had a foreign exchange student from Italy. I walked into one of my classes and noticed that she was sitting all alone. Instances like this broke my heart, so I sat next to her and made her feel welcome. I knew to a certain degree what it felt like to be different and to be in new surroundings, not knowing anyone.

Even though I lived in emotional pain, I always enjoyed putting a smile on someone else's face, especially my family members. Seeing someone else smile filled me with joy. I was full of surprises. One time, I worked with my family to surprise my mom for Mother's Day by taking her to see one of her favorite performers. I coordinated everything, including purchasing the concert tickets and arranging the hotel reservation.

The reveal day arrived! We shared with my mom where we were going to take her, and excitement filled the room. Little did I know that the concert that evening would be a stepping stone and a tremendous encouragement for me as well.

The concert began, and about forty-five minutes into the artist's performance, she stopped in the middle of the song and said, "I don't know who this is for, but the Holy Spirit has laid something on my heart that I need to share with you all. At a young age, I was abused sexually."

My ears perked up immediately. The thoughts that often bounced around my mind, such as *"You won't amount to anything"* and *"You brought this on yourself,"* became silent. I was completely tuned in to what she was about to say. She went on to share some of her innermost feelings, including the insecurities she felt growing up as a result of the abuse.

Tears formed in my eyes. I knew that God was speaking through her directly to me. Every word she spoke resonated in my spirit, letting me know that I was not alone and that there were others just like her out in the world who had faced a similar experience. She was the first person in my life to whom I could truly relate. Her story comforted me and reassured me that God could still use me. I knew then for the first time in my life that I could go on to make something of myself, just like she did as a well-known professional singer. The words she spoke encouraged me to continue pressing forward even though I ached inwardly.

As I entered high school, the abuse eventually ended because I just stopped going over to my friend's house, not caring at that point what consequences might follow. The father of my friend would sometimes drop by my house to check in on my family. Anytime I saw him arrive, I went into my room and stayed there until he left because I couldn't stand to see him. The verbal bullying started to minimize as well at that point, but overall I had deeply rooted wounds, was insecure, and lacked confidence.

I was so ready for graduation, in part to move on and to prove to the world that I was going to make something of myself (though I learned later in life that I didn't have anything to prove). More importantly, I needed to get away from my current environment because everywhere I turned, I had constant reminders of my inner pain.

My father decided to resign from the pastoral role in my early years of high school. As a family, we started attending a local church that was a good size and had multiple services. It was the first time in a while that it was more than just my siblings and I who made up the youth group. It was a much-needed change for not only me, but the entire family.

In the summer between my sophomore and junior years, I attended a youth conference at the Denver Convention Center. Typically, I would write speakers off as soon as they started talking. Either I wouldn't be intrigued or entertained by what they were saying, or they would preach a message I couldn't bear to listen to. I would immediately tune out when I heard, "You need to do this or that," or, "God doesn't want you to be like this." I would wonder, *"What have these people been through in their lives that gives them the right to stand there and tell me what I should or should not be doing?"*

However, something caught my attention when this speaker started sharing the illustration of the empty bottle and the bottle full of golf balls, which represented the circumstances we encounter and whether or not we choose to carry them with us throughout our lives. The empty bottle had more room for the sand, which signified the time and opportunities we are given. I couldn't simply forget about what happened to me, but I knew that somehow, someway, if I pressed forward to the goal ahead of me, God would use it all for His purpose and His glory.

CHAPTER FOURTEEN

A Bundle of Support

So do not fear, for I am with you; do not be dismayed, for I am your God. I will strengthen you and help you; I will uphold you with my righteous right hand.
—Isaiah 41:10 *(NIV)*

Less than a month after my first consultation at Cleveland Clinic, my mother and I were back for our third visit. I was shuffled from one location of the hospital to another during the full day of autonomic testing. I was physically and mentally drained from the travel back and forth, the testing, and the past that still hung on my shoulders.

Every doctor to whom I was referred wanted to conduct his or her own tests. My body had been poked and prodded frequently over the last year and a half. My college years were slipping through my fingers as I lay there, looking at yet another ceiling. The medical staff began inserting different types of dyes into my body as they ran multiple scans and several tilt table tests.

Later that afternoon, once the testing had concluded, the doctor sat down to review the results with us. I was informed that I had inappropriate sinus tachycardia (which we already knew) and that it was linked to postural orthostatic tachycardia syndrome, also known as POTS. The doctor went on to explain that POTS affects the circulation (blood flow) and involves both the autonomic nervous system and the sympathetic nervous system. With this condition, too little blood flow returns to the heart when someone moves from a lying position to a standing position. As a result, there is a rapid increase in heart rate, and the person may become lightheaded or even faint. Episodes often begin after major surgery or trauma, both of which I had recently experienced.[10]

All of the information the doctor provided made sense. There had been so many times when I had experienced lightheadedness, feeling like I was about to faint, but couldn't put my finger on what was causing it. The doctor put me on a high-salt-intake diet and increased my beta-blocker medicine to help offset the increase in heart rate and help to prevent lightheadedness and fainting. The good news was that in most cases, the disorder eventually goes away. *"Let's just hope so,"* I thought.

While I wasn't yet cured of my heart issues, I was glad for the clarity regarding what was happening. I was informed that I would need to continue having follow-ups with my cardiologist on a regular basis but would no longer need to return to Cleveland.

I was starting to see why doctors were initially stating that

I had a very complex case. The car accident resulted in extensive internal injuries. The imbalance of my upper extremities (shoulder/thoracic area) caused a lot of other functions of my body to be impacted over time. Piece by piece, day by day, we were getting more answers to what was causing my symptoms.

My mother and I drove back to Defiance later that evening. I had planned to stay a few days over the Christmas holiday before heading back to Dallas. One evening, I wrote the following in my journal:

> Journal Entry (Wednesday, Dec 30, 2004): It has been nice being home with family for the past few days over my Christmas break. Last night, I opened up to my sister, my best friend, regarding what had happened to me as a child. Ever since I was six years old, when the abuse started, I had been hiding this from everyone. I feel a sense of further release, a burden being lifted, now that someone besides me in this family knows what happened. Christina said that she was sorry and told me, "David, I don't know why you have had to go through so much." I thought to myself later, *"I don't know, either, but God does, and He will use my testimony in some way."*

Three Months Later

In March, I headed home for a few days over spring break. One evening, my mom, my dad, and I were all together in the kitchen area, and somehow we got on the subject of what had happened to me as a kid. I was shocked but, at the same time, a little relieved that they had already found out about the abuse. I wasn't sure how that conversation would have gone if I'd had to inform them myself. They had found out through a series of events but didn't want to bring it up until I was home.

We conversed back and forth regarding what had happened. I was thankful that they had processed their emotions prior to having the conversation with me. I pretended that I was okay. I was working through it, or at least I thought I was. I had already had a conversation with a friend about what had happened, and I thought that would be it. I wanted to release the baggage but didn't really know how to deal with it properly.

I knew that my parents were sincerely sorry about what had happened and felt bad that I had suffered in this way. They offered to pay for counseling, but I thought that talking to someone about my past wouldn't help. I brushed it all under me, gave them a hug, and told them that I loved them.

The remaining days at home flew by, and before long, I was back in Dallas, hitting the books again. Over the next few months, I continued with school, work, and my follow-up appointments as needed in Houston. Before I knew it, another semester was under my belt.

Overall, my health had improved, but I was still having the episodes of rapidly increasing heart rate as well as intense spasticity in my lower legs. I was taking ten to twelve pills a day of the muscle-relaxer medicine I was on.

My mother and I headed back to Houston on Monday, May 23, this time for a test dose of intrathecal baclofen that would be inserted into my spine during a spinal tap procedure. It was a fairly new test and was being issued to see if I would qualify for a Medtronic infusion pump.

After the procedure was finished, Dr. Loftus got me up off the bed and took me around the hospital on a long walk. I went up and down multiple flights of stairs. For the first time since the accident, my legs felt normal! He tested my reflexes back in the examine room and noticed how much of a difference it had made.

Later that day, he informed us that I was a candidate for this procedure. The downside would be that I would need to have the medical device surgically implanted and would require a surgery every five to seven years for the rest of my life to replace the device, along with medication refill procedures every two months. The upside would be that I would likely be completely off the muscle-relaxer medicine that I was taking orally, a medication that constantly made my body tired. This other option would be more targeted, strategically placed where I needed it to go (my lower extremities). After careful consideration and prayer, I decided to move forward with the surgery based on how well the results had turned out, and I began making plans for the procedure.

Knowing that I would have another summer break that would be consumed with treatment, I talked it over with the college and made arrangements to stay on campus in the dorm. This would allow me not to have to worry about taking all of my stuff home, only to return a few short months later. While the process had been hard on me, I was very grateful to be attending a college that helped to lighten the load I had on my shoulders. I was surrounded by professors and students who truly cared and were doing their best to help me through this season of my life.

> Journal Entry (Wednesday, July 13, 2005): I will be flying back out to Houston tomorrow for my next surgery. It is hard to believe that another summer break is quickly flying by.
>
> I received the biggest care package today from my home church back in Ohio (Free Christian Church of God). It was filled to the brim with personal, handwritten letters from different youth students and members of the church (many of whom I did not know).
>
> Here are just a few:
>
> *Dear David,*
>
> *Just want you to know that you have been in our prayers and will continue to be. I want you to know that our church is praying, too. I keep everyone updated every time your mom calls me. I don't understand why God is allowing this to happen to you, but always remember that He is in control. You are where He is allowing you to be. You have been through so much. I don't understand how you can get up every morning feeling the way you do. Most people would have given up by now. You have been such an inspiration to so many of us. But when you feel down, remember Isaiah 41:10. God is watching over you, David. You are His child, and He loves you. We all do. Keep this prayer cloth with you.*
>
> *Dear David,*
>
> *I want to start off by saying that I am so sorry. No one should have to go through this. When I get down, I look at this verse—Philippians 4:13. It is my favorite verse, and I remember that God is always there. I know you are going through something that is bringing you down. I know you*

want to give up. But remember that everyone is praying for you, wanting you to get through this. God has bigger, better things waiting for you. Trust that God will help you. My family and I will be praying for you.

Looking back over the last few years, I can see that I have been blessed with a great support system. God, You have given both my family and me incredible people on this difficult journey who have stood by us and supported us by providing encouragement and, most importantly, prayer. I have received constant encouraging text messages and cards, and people have shown up to my surgeries just to let me know that they care.

Father, thank You for each of them. You know them all by name, and I'm grateful for them. I know their prayers are keeping us going!

Here We Go Again

I was once again being wheeled back to the OR at the Methodist hospital in Houston, this time for the surgical implant of the intrathecal infusion pump. It was late in the afternoon. My surgery had been pushed back to a start time of 3 p.m. on Friday due to several surgeries prior to mine taking much longer than anticipated. The neurosurgeon came in and acknowledged that he was in the room prior to me being put to sleep.

Several hours later, I woke up in the recovery room. I had an extreme amount of pain. My abdominal area had several inches of incisions where a medical device had been forced in under the skin and the skin had been stretched over the device and then stapled shut. On my back side, the catheter had been placed in my spine and then enclosed with staples. The medical device would carry medication internally from the device through inner tubing directly into my spine so that it would be more targeted to the area where I needed it.

Lying there in the hospital bed, I felt so bad. Any movement whatsoever caused even more discomfort. With incisions in my abdominal area and on the back side, I couldn't find a comfortable spot. Throughout the late evening and into the night, I periodically dozed off to sleep, typically after a round of pain medicine, but it wouldn't be long before I woke up due to the pain returning.

Around 7 a.m., my bed was raised up a few inches so I would be in more of a sitting position. Shortly thereafter, I developed a headache that seemed to get progressively worse as the minutes ticked away. Not long after 9 a.m., I had an extreme headache to the point where I couldn't stand it, and I was feeling very nauseous.

I had visitors that day, but I didn't feel up to carrying on a conversation. I felt so bad all over, and my headache only continued to get worse.

"Mom," I whispered. Struggling to get the words out, I leaned over and said, "I don't feel well. I think I'm about to get sick."

She immediately told my dad to grab a pail, but he wasn't quick enough. Suddenly, I began to vomit uncontrollably all over the bed and floor, with only a few seconds of pause before the next round would project out with intensity.

I lay there in misery. I held a pillow against my stomach, trying to apply some pressure and support to the incisions I had in my abdominal area. Every time I projected the vomit out, I ached to a level that I had never experienced before.

I continued to vomit even though I had very little in my stomach. I cried and pleaded for relief as I lay there. My head was pounding so badly, and the pain only intensified.

My body continued to convulse with dry heaves as I lay in a fetal position on the hospital bed, feeling hopeless and wondering how much longer I could go on like this. I continued praying, asking God to take the pain away. The pressure in my head magnified to the point where I couldn't think clearly.

The on-floor doctor prescribed different medicines, none of which helped. My bed was lowered when they determined that I had a CSF leak, a post-surgery complication in which cerebrospinal fluid leaks out of the spinal cord and causes headaches that worsen when the person sits or stands.

At around 7 p.m., I was put on morphine and additional nausea medicine. My bed would remain completely flat until the pressure subsided and the spinal leak was able to seal itself, which would take time. As I lay there, looking at the ceiling of the hospital room, I wondered, *"Did I make the right choice in having this surgery?"* Soon I fell asleep, only to be awoken by the nurse who came in every hour or so to check vitals and bandages.

By mid-morning on Sunday, the pressure in my head had improved as the spinal leak was starting to seal, and I was able to keep a little food in my stomach. Throughout the morning, I lay there on the bed with my sister next to me, and we watched TV. Around 12 p.m., we decided to start raising my bed an inch every few hours so that my body would gradually adjust and the spinal leak could continue to improve.

Just after 2 p.m., my dad and sister got ready to leave for the airport. They were going to fly back home that evening. Given that I was improving, I told them to go ahead since I knew that my Dad needed to get back to work. I gave them hugs, and my Dad spoke a prayer over me before my mom took them to the airport.

While my mom was away, I watched TV in my hospital room, and I saw that Houston was preparing for a hurricane that was scheduled to hit on Tuesday afternoon. It had already been an intense weekend, and I couldn't begin to think of us having to deal with a hurricane as well.

Throughout the evening, I gradually started to feel better, though my head still hurt. I could only stand for my bed to be up for a short period of time before having to lower it again, which would give me relief from the pounding headache. Doctors informed me that it could take a few days or even weeks before I would be able to sit up fully and no longer have the headaches.

Monday morning came around, and my neurologist, Dr. Loftus, called to check on me. He was shocked to find that I was still in the hospital. Most patients were released within twenty-four hours of the surgery, yet here I was, going into my third day in the hospital. He came down over his lunch hour after my mom informed him of what was going on. He walked into my room and asked how I was doing.

"Much better," I responded.

He tested my legs to see how the spasticity was and then

adjusted the medication in my device. Before leaving, he said, "Hang in there. I expect to see you in my office in a few days."

I smiled back at him and responded, "Will do."

After he left, I asked the on-floor doctor if I could be released since I was doing better. I wanted to get to our hotel room, knowing that both my mom and I could use a good night's rest. He agreed and told me to continue working on sitting up for as long as I could stand it before lying down flat again. He promised that it would eventually get better, but timing varied for each patient with a CSF leak.

Later that afternoon, my mom had settled me in the comfort of a hotel room. We would be staying there for the next week until my staples were removed and all of my follow-up appointments had been completed.

Once she had me all settled, my mom went out to get some food for us. Shortly after she returned, the rain started pouring down outside. I was so grateful that we were already inside and not having to deal with the storm while being discharged, and I thanked God in my prayers before I drifted off to sleep.

A Bundle of Support

Within a week, I was starting to get up and about, still sore but doing well overall after the surgery. My humor returned, and my response to anyone who asked how I was doing was: "I'm doing cartwheels at home." I wasn't really doing cartwheels, of course, but it was a saying I had used from the beginning to let my family and friends know that I was okay and could still keep some humor in all of this.

Once the staples had been removed and the medication set to the proper dose, my mom and I flew back to Ohio so I could recover at home. Soon after I arrived back home, my mom received a call from one of our family friends letting her know that our local church and high school were going to throw me a benefit in September to help raise funds for all of my expenses. It was such a kind gesture, one that I knew we all needed.

I returned to Dallas in the middle of August after a few weeks of recovery. I was back for less than a month before returning home for the benefit. Billboards with my picture were up all around town to advertise the benefit. The fundraiser included numerous events, which would all be held at the local high school from which I had graduated only two years earlier.

In poured people from all over Ayersville and Defiance, some of whom I knew and others I didn't, all to support my family and me. As I looked around, I saw people I had gone to school with, coaches, teachers, church members, and some complete strangers, all rallying behind a cause.

As I sat in the cafeteria and observed my surroundings, a couple of things dawned on me. All those years I had attended this school, I came to this cafeteria day in and day out to eat. God knew every time I sat down in these seats that I would be back after graduation. Even in the midst of this difficult journey, He was always there, loving me, guiding me, and protecting me.

I also realized how big of a platform He had placed me on.

So many people had looked up to me and prayed for me throughout this journey. I had the opportunity in this moment as I took the stage at the benefit and beyond to share my faith and gratitude, speak words of encouragement, and testify to the power of perseverance.

As I looked out over all those who attended the benefit, they reminded me of the value of friendship and how human hearts truly need each other. It was this large community, their support and prayers, that was helping my family and me to take one step after another on this difficult journey.

CHAPTER FIFTEEN

A Mother's Cry

These things I have spoken to you, that in Me you may have peace. In the world you will have tribulation; but be of good cheer, I have overcome the world.
—John 16:33 *(NKJV)*

KELLY ROSE, MOTHER OF DAVID
Sharing the Journey to This Point Through Her Eyes

Tears of joy trickled down my face as the nurses placed my baby son in my arms on a cold Sunday afternoon in December. The pain, anguish, and uncertainty that had bounced around my mind during the long delivery process was soon replaced with joy as I held him tightly in my arms. I will never forget my doctor's reaction. He was thrilled because my son was the biggest baby he had ever delivered: 10 pounds, 14 ounces.

"Sign this baby up for the Cincinnati Bengals!" the doctor

declared excitedly.

I smiled, cherishing the moment, as my baby lay in my arms and my husband stood right there next to me. Shortly afterwards, the nurse picked up my son from my arms so that he could be taken into another room for all of the examinations.

Hours passed. It was 7 p.m. when a doctor walked into my room with a somber look on his face.

"Your son has been transferred to the Pediatrics Intensive Care Unit," the doctor told me. "In our examination, your son had some difficulty breathing. After running several tests, we uncovered that he has a spot on his lungs. To be honest, we don't know what it is. We'll continue to monitor him and run different tests as needed."

As the doctor walked out of the room, the news hit me like a bag of bricks. The joy and excitement of my son's arrival was suddenly replaced with fear and uncertainty. I wanted to see him, to hold him in my arms and tell him that it was all going to be okay. But was it?

Due to my baby's condition, I couldn't see him. I lay in my hospital room all night, just thinking about him and praying for him. I prayed, *"God, heal my son. Thank You for the plans that You have for him."*

The following morning, I was told that I could see David. Due to his condition, I had to be fully gowned up and put on gloves before I could enter his room. They wheeled me in to see him. It was hard to see my baby boy enclosed in an incubator with an IV inserted into his forehead. I couldn't hold him, so I put my arm through the little hand opening in the incubator and began to rub his arm and his back as I whispered words of encouragement to him. I sat there for hours, singing to him and loving on him.

I was informed later that evening that I would be released in the morning because insurance would not approve for me to be in the hospital any longer. Deep down, I wanted to stay. In the wee hours of the morning, I started having it out with the Lord. I didn't understand why this was happening.

Around 2 a.m., I heard a knock at the door. An ICU doctor came into my room and sat down next to me in a chair. "Ma'am," he said. "We don't know what is wrong with your son. Chest X-rays show a spot on his lungs. In my years of practice, I have never seen anything like it before. We're treating him with aggressive antibiotics and will continue to monitor him. I know you will be released later this morning, but I want you to know that I will personally call you every morning to give you an update on the status of your son."

I thanked him as he walked out of my room. His calm and optimistic demeanor had comforted me.

Gary came to the hospital around 10 a.m. on Tuesday, December 4, and we packed up my things. Before we left the hospital, we both went in to see our son. We loved on him, knowing that he needed that more than anything else.

Later that afternoon, my husband dropped me off at my parents' house before he started his drive back to Kentucky. He had received the calling to be a minister a few months earlier, and he was beginning his education. I was staying with my parents until we could all make the move down to Kentucky together once David was released.

That evening and into the early morning hours, there was a terrible snowstorm. My father-in-law knew how determined I was to see my son in the hospital, so he spent some time that morning putting the tire chains on the car. The doctor lived up to his promise and called me that morning. He told me that there wasn't any change in David's condition and that they would keep monitoring him as they continued with antibiotics.

My father-in-law picked me up at my parents' house and took me to the hospital. I stayed there with my son all day as my father-in-law waited patiently in the lobby area.

I called my husband and provided an update on how David was doing. He informed me that he had requested prayer there on campus and that the president of the college had found out about our son's condition and had called for a prayer vigil to be held later that evening.

The following morning, I received a call from my husband. He told me that the prayer vigil had been standing-room only. The chapel had been packed wall-to-wall with people praying specifically for the healing of our son.

An hour or so after getting off the phone with my husband, I received a call from the doctor.

"Ma'am," he said, "I don't know how to explain it to you, but we took an additional X-ray this morning, and the spot was still on his lung. Something told me to run the X-ray again, so I had the technician do so. The lungs were as clear as could be. I had him run it one more time. Once again, the lungs were as healthy as could be. I can't explain it. All I can say is that your baby is healed. We'll plan to go ahead and release him tomorrow morning. I suggest that once you come to get him, you take him immediately to whatever home you plan to raise him in so his body can adjust to that."

I hung up the phone, tears of joy and amazement rolling down my face. *"The power of prayer,"* I thought.

I called my husband to tell him the great news. Excitement filled the line as we conversed. He said that he would leave first thing the next morning to pick us up.

David was released the following morning, and we made our way down to our new home in Kentucky. For the record, David never had any further issues pertaining to the function of his lungs.

Eighteen Years Later

The phone rang around 11:30 p.m. Our daughter picked it up. I heard a knock at the door shortly thereafter, and my daughter walked in and handed me the phone.

"David is on the line," she said.

I was a little groggy when I answered because I had recently fallen asleep.

"Mom, I was in a pretty bad accident, but I'm okay," I heard over the phone as my youngest son talked on the other line. The grogginess was soon replaced with an adrenaline rush. My heart started to beat faster and faster. It was the news that every parent dreads to hear. I felt fearful, just as I had when a doctor had informed me that something was wrong with David soon after he was born. I didn't know if my son was okay. My mind fluttered with different thoughts as I waited for another call from him. In the meantime, I hurried into another room to tell my husband, who hadn't gone to bed yet.

We began packing our bags and were prepared to drive all through the night to get to Dallas. I was thinking the worst.

David later called me and told me that he was back in his dorm room and was okay. I was relieved somewhat, but I lay there all night, wondering if he was truly okay.

A few weeks later, I flew to Dallas for David's appointment with a specialist. I will never forget how the person sitting next to me on the plane asked me if I was okay. He likely sensed how tense I was. I shared that my son had recently been involved in a hit-and-run car accident. I didn't know what to expect in terms of the shape his body would be in, how I would react to seeing him, or what the course of the next few days would hold for us.

I walked through the circular, spinning glass doors at DFW International Airport, and there stood my son. His body was severely off balance. It was as if his right shoulder had completely collapsed. He looked weak and pale. I walked up to him and hugged him. It was good to have him back in my arms. I started to tear up as David whispered to me, "I'm okay, mom. We're going to get through this together."

The months ahead were filled with every emotion one could ever imagine. As a mother, I ached inwardly at a level that I couldn't quite convey to anyone else. Constantly seeing my son go through so much pain was almost unbearably difficult. No matter how old he got, he was still my baby boy, and I longed to see him get well. I did everything I could to take his mind off the current situation, wishing that I was the one bearing this burden instead of him.

The hardest part as a mother was the distance between us. While I was present for every procedure and surgery, there were so many nights when I would receive a call from either a friend of David's or a doctor telling me that David had been rushed to a hospital or his condition was getting worse. I felt like I was living in a bubble, just waiting for the next big collision to occur.

I spent my days between my bus routes on the phone with hospital medical billing and our health insurance company, sorting through what needed to be paid. The stress and worry of the bills piling up and wondering how we were going to pay them with the tight budget we lived on was always running through my mind.

As a mother, I was pulled in a million directions. One moment, I was hopping on another plane to head to another doctor's appointment. Then I was caring for my son as he endured another procedure or surgery. All the while, I had to keep up with the housework, my job, and most importantly, my family. My daughter was in the prime of her high-school years. Often my husband and I would have to decide who would attend what. We tried to provide some normalcy for the family during this season, but deep down, the journey was taking a tremendous toll on all of us.

The complexity of David's injuries added another layer of worry and stress not only on him, but also on the family. So many times, we walked into the office of a particular specialist who was supposed to be one of the best and, after he had looked at David's records, would hear something along the lines of: "I haven't seen anything like this since med school," or, "Let me refer you to another surgeon or specialist." As a mother, I was always proud to see David continuing to press forward although, at times, it seemed as if there weren't any answers or good news in sight.

I will never forget the morning when David was being prepped for the rib-removal surgery. The cardiothoracic surgeon, Dr. Urschel, asked a neurosurgeon to come in and evaluate David's neck right before taking him back to the operating room. They stepped out into the hallway and had a very heated conversation about my son's case. Afterwards, Dr. Urschel walked in and motioned for the medical team to take David off to surgery. As my son was wheeled down the hallway, the tears that I had held back to be strong for him started running down my face. It was as if my heart were being pulled out from within me. *"Are we making the right decision?"* I asked myself. Shortly thereafter, Dr. Urschel came up to me. He didn't say a word, just patted me on the back. This is a small glimpse of the worry and anguish that coursed constantly through my mind as a mother.

The difficult season continued to unfold in the year ahead as David went on to endure additional procedures and surgeries. When I felt that I was at a point where I couldn't bear anything else, I found out through a series of events that my son had been abused sexually as a child. It seemed for a moment that everything just stopped. I was devastated.

I heard a knock at the door not long after I found out what had happened to my son as a child. A friend of mine, Betty (the mother of Alexandra, the teenager who was hospitalized when David was a senior in high school and whom we went to visit often), had stopped by the house to check in on me and to see how David was doing. My husband opened the door. I was a basket case, crying my heart out in the other room, and didn't want to come out and have Betty see me this way. My husband knew the friend that she was to us and encouraged me to come out and share what had happened since she had stopped by specifically to see me. After much encouragement, I opened up to her and shared what I had just found out. Betty had been a rock to me throughout David's ordeal. At that moment, the timing of her visit had seemed so imperfect, but looking back now, I can see that she was the shoulder I needed to cry on and the sister I needed to speak words of encouragement to me as a mother.

Those years had more down days than good ones, but in those difficult times, I witnessed God's hand guiding us through the process and using David and our family to be a light in a season of uncertainty. I wasn't sure how God was going to use David in the next chapter of his life, but I believed that He had a plan for all of his suffering. David's giving, caring, and compassionate heart toward others only grew through all of this, and I was looking forward to seeing what God had in store for him next.

CHAPTER SIXTEEN

Finding a Purpose

You intended to harm me, but God intended it for good to accomplish what is now being done....
                                        —*Genesis 50:20 (NIV)*

Overall, my health had improved, and I was primarily in the care of my neurologist and cardiologist. I continued to have doctor's appointments and trips back and forth to Houston while juggling schoolwork and a job.

On my journey so far, I had spent countless hours in hospital rooms, seeing numerous doctors and surgeons in various fields, and had endured a great deal of physical pain as well as personal expense. Too many hours, days, and months had been consumed with all of this. During those difficult days, I would wonder about the person behind the wheel of the car that hit me on October 24 and kept going. What was that person up to? Did he or she have any remorse over what had happened? Did the person have any idea of how much he or she had changed my life?

I also often thought about how I could turn this bad situation into something positive. Over the past few years, I had seen so many children alongside me in the hospitals and doctors' offices enduring similar health issues. I asked God, *"What can I do to help?"* Over the course of my journey, God laid it upon my heart to start a nonprofit organization to uplift and encourage children and their families with medical-related needs. I knew firsthand how challenging the past few years had been for me. The pain and the constant bad news sometimes led me to ask myself, *"Is life worth living?"* I knew full well how much of a toll seeking medical care could take not only on the patient, but also on the family, and how each member of the family gives up so much in the process. Through my own journey, I had been so blessed to have an amazing support system, and I recalled how the cards and encouraging texts gave me the motivation to keep going.

When I asked God for a name for the organization, "To Give A Smile" came to mind. Our focus would be on giving children a reason to smile in the midst of their current health situation through fun and uplifting activities. At the time, I didn't have a clue how to run a nonprofit organization, but I knew deep down that God had given me direction and was going to use the trials that I had endured for a greater purpose.

I set out to recruit a team, which initially included my sister, Christina, and a good friend of mine named Rhonda. I had the vision, and I moved forward with it. People in my circle and even complete strangers tried to discourage me from beginning the journey. I knew that many of them had the best intentions. They were trying to protect me from any legal ramifications that could come from launching an organization. With a determined mind, I set out at the age of 20 to begin the process of building the organization.

Initially, I thought that the vision would materialize quickly. I had pictured in my mind what I thought the organization would become, but I learned quickly that the process often takes time. In the coming months, whenever I could squeeze it into my schedule, I met with different people whom God brought along to help us with establishing the organization, including paperwork, the financial structure that needed to be in place, and so forth. Before long, we submitted the 501(c) paperwork. Months later, we got the approval.

My time was somewhat limited. I was working full time at a local hotel to help pay the medical bills, travel-related costs, and my personal living expenses. I had recently shifted over to evening classes as that seemed to work best for my schedule. Doing so gave me the flexibility during the day to work if needed, attend doctor's appointments, get caught up on my studies, and meet with any people I needed to in order to establish the organization. A professor of mine who started off as a mentor and became a good friend recommended the evening classes. He had always been supportive and encouraging, yet he didn't cut me any slack in the process, for which I was grateful.

Over time, the organization raised enough money to create a website, and we hosted our first outreach. Rhonda,

Christina, and I met up in Memphis, Tennessee, and hosted our first event at the Ronald McDonald House near the St. Jude Hospital. We prepared and served a meal, followed by an activity with the kids. As I sat there, watching smiles light up the faces of these innocent children who were going through one of life's most difficult seasons, I knew that I was in the place I needed to be. I didn't quite know how God was going to use To Give A Smile, but I knew that He had me on this journey for a reason.

On the flight back to Dallas the next day, I had a flashback to my senior year of high school when someone had asked me, "What do you want to do with your life?" I recalled how I had responded, stating that I would love to be a part of some type of nonprofit and be a motivational speaker. It dawned on me that here I was, five years later, branching off and building a nonprofit that would encourage children and their families who were enduring medical hardships. The scripture that came to mind was 2 Corinthians 1:3–4 (NKJV):

Blessed be the God and Father of our Lord Jesus Christ, the Father of mercies and God of all comfort, who comforts us in all our tribulation, that we may be able to comfort those who are in any trouble, with the comfort with which we ourselves are comforted by God.

God gave me these experiences that enabled me to understand how difficult the process of seeking medical care could be so that I could help comfort others enduring similar circumstances.

One day, I stumbled across a website that showed a statistic on how many children died each year of preventable causes due to lack of basic medical care. My sister had a passion for healthcare and was planning to go into the medical field after graduation. We conversed, and the entire team agreed that we were also meant to carry the mission internationally and take medical care to those who needed it. I believe that God directs our paths in the way He wants us to go, and I couldn't shake off those staggering numbers. I placed the future of the organization in His hands and believed that He would bring about the work He intended us to do internationally in His timing.

Throughout the year, the organization continued with different activities in local hospitals and Ronald McDonald Houses. Our activities included delivering toys to children, cooking meals, and building crafts with the kids to take back to their rooms. The goal was simply to take children's minds off all they were going through and, for a short period, allow them to be kids again despite all they were facing.

Every smile that a child gave me or one of our volunteers after receiving a toy, the sound of laughter when the children were enjoying our games, and the simple "thank you" for a meal we provided put the biggest smile on my heart. I knew, to a certain degree, what these kids were going through. Many of them were in the biggest fight of their lives, and they needed community, love, and support. I realized then that though the accident was intended to harm me, it turned out to be the biggest blessing of my life in disguise.

CHAPTER SEVENTEEN

A New Beginning

So I say to you: Ask and it will be given to you; seek and you will find; knock and the door will be opened to you. For everyone who asks receives; the one who seeks finds; and to the one who knocks, the door will be opened.
—Luke 11:9–10 (NIV)

In the fall of my junior year of college, I had the opportunity to transition to another hotel. A previous Director of Sales recruited me over. Not long after I started, I quickly moved up into management, helping to run a 24/7 hotel that was less than two miles from the Dallas/Fort Worth International Airport. There was never a dull moment in the hotel; it was always busy. We never knew when we would get a call from the airlines to inform us that a flight was canceled, in which case we would go from a low-end occupancy to a fully sold-out hotel within minutes. I enjoyed the thrill and the busyness, and the job seemed to work well with my college schedule.

After less than six months of being at the hotel, I was presented an opportunity to transition to another property that was managed and operated by the same company. After giving it plenty of thought, I decided to move forward with the opportunity, showing the company that I was willing to grow in my career and be flexible.

During this time, I started getting a few speaking opportunities at various churches. I was excited, thinking that it was the beginning of the motivational speaking that God had placed on my heart back when I was in high school. At one of the speaking events, before I took the stage, the elders of the church surrounded me and began to pray over me. They spoke words of encouragement and asked God to speak through me. Shortly thereafter, I was up on stage, talking to a large audience. I was privileged to share my testimony and speak of how God had given me the strength to get through the difficult season I had recently experienced. Afterwards, many in the congregation shook my hand and told me how my story had touched them personally before they exited the building.

Opportunities continued to come for speaking events in the months ahead, but I eventually stopped accepting the invitations. Deep down, I wasn't truly healed, and I realized that I needed to take care of myself before pouring into others. I still didn't truly know what healing looked like for me. Outwardly, my physical body was better, but I still ached inside.

I continued through my education, knowing that the end was within reach, and my hours at the hotel increased. It seemed like my cell phone was always ringing, making it hard to have any life whatsoever outside of work.

One day, I was driving the hotel van, and on my route, I dropped someone off at a building that turned out to be the corporate office for a major hotel company. I began to consider how a corporate office setting might be a better fit for me. The job would have set hours, which would allow me the time to finish school, grow the nonprofit organization, and have a life outside of work.

Every time I went to work, I drove by that corporate building. I would point to the building and say, "I'm going to work there someday." I bound it in prayer and began circling and declaring it. I soon applied for a job. I made it to the second round of interviews, only to find out that I didn't get the job. It was a blow to my ego. I questioned for a moment but then reminded myself to keep trying.

Months passed, and no jobs I was remotely interested in appeared on the site. I continued with my current job, getting more frustrated with the number of hours I was putting in. During this time, my right hip started to cause me a great deal of pain. I was standing on my feet at the front desk for eight to ten hours at a time. I blew the pain off for a while, tired of seeing doctors and going through procedures.

As the days went by, I continued to check the website of the corporate office. One day, a position opened that seemed to be a good fit for me. I applied for it and continued to pray. A few days later, I got a call from the department to which I had applied. I went through the series of interviews and once again was informed that I had interviewed well but they had decided to go with another candidate. I was back to square one again. I started asking God, *"Is this where You want me to go?"*

The pain in my hip continued to intensify to the point where I could no longer put off dealing with it. I decided to call and make an appointment. I thought back to the doctors whom I had visited in the last few years to see if there was anyone in their same practices who specialized in orthopedics. Then I remembered Dr. Graehl, the first specialist to whom I was referred by Dr. Dodge. He was an orthopedic surgeon who had agreed to see me at the beginning of my journey and then referred me to Dr. Frazier, the spine specialist.

I called the doctor's office and scheduled an appointment for a couple of weeks out. In the meantime, I decided to check the hotel corporate website again to see if any positions had become available. Sure enough, there was a position available in the first department to which I had applied. As I read through the responsibilities, this position seemed to be even more intriguing and a better fit for me than the first one I had interviewed for, so I applied.

A few days later, I got a call to schedule an interview. They had an opportunity available the next day, so I went ahead and took it. That evening, I mentally prepared answers to the questions I thought they might ask.

When I arrived the next morning, I went into the lobby area. I didn't have my hopes up, but I reminded myself to do my best. Soon someone came to get me and took me back to an office. When I entered, I saw the panel of people who would be interviewing me. I was asked different questions and felt confident that the interview was going well. At the end, they asked if I had any questions. I went through my questions and closed by asking when I should expect an update. They told me that they were working through interviews with a few candidates and should have an update in the next two weeks.

Later in the week, I sat in the lobby of Dr. Graehl's office. It was hard to believe that I had come full circle to where I had begun my journey of seeking medical answers a few years prior. Shortly after arriving, my name was called. Dr. Graehl examined me and told me that he wanted to order an MRI, which would be scheduled at a nearby imaging center.

Several days later, after completing the MRI, I was back in Dr. Graehl's office. The test revealed that the bone was not fitting into the socket properly, and the cartilage was torn, which required another surgery. He stated that if I didn't proceed with the operation, I would likely need a full hip replacement within a year or two. I asked him if he thought that it was related to the car accident. He said that there was a good chance it could be, but he couldn't say for certain. I scheduled the surgery for a couple of weeks later, though I was not looking forward to another operation.

A new general manager started at the hotel where I worked, and he was doing things that I didn't think were right. I filed a complaint with the main office regarding things he was doing that I considered unethical. I still hadn't received any update on the position I had interviewed for at the corporate office, but I took a leap of faith and resigned from my position. I had built up some savings and decided that I didn't need the stress of the job. I was going to give it to God to direct my steps.

Over the next two weeks leading up to the surgery, I looked for other positions and spent time in God's Word and in prayer. My parents and sister flew in a few days before the operation, so we had some time to hang out as a family.

Before long, I was once again being prepped for a surgery. The operation lasted a few hours, and I was released the same day. My dad and sister left to head back home while my mom stayed with me in Dallas for a few more days.

As I was lying on the couch one day, recovering from the operation, I received a call from a number I didn't recognize. I had applied for some positions, so I decided to take it. Come to find it was the corporate office for the large hotel company calling me to offer the job that I had interviewed for six weeks before. I was so happy, and I knew that the job offer was an answer to my prayers. We discussed compensation and the start date, which I scheduled for just over two weeks later because I was going to fly back home with my mom to attend my sister's graduation.

A week went by, and I built up some strength, though being on crutches sure drained my energy. My mom and I headed back home to start preparing for my sister's big day and graduation party. The week seemed to fly by. Before long, I saw my sister walk up to receive her diploma, which marked another moment in my life that I was privileged and grateful to be there to witness.

Two days later, my sister and I flew back to Dallas. She was going to stay with me for a couple of weeks and help me around the apartment since I was on crutches and was limited in what I could do. I started my workweek at the corporate office. I was excited to be branching into a new career that would provide good benefits and a set schedule, something I realized that I needed more than ever.

Over the summer, I found out through my adviser at school that I would need to complete a couple more classes, which would push back my graduation. Instead of finishing in May of 2007, I would finish up the following December and would walk in May of 2008. While I wanted to be done, I was okay with my current pace. Trying to pile on more classes just to finish more quickly didn't make sense to me.

After a few months had passed, I was officially beginning my senior year of college. I kept dreaming of the day when I could be done with classes completely.

The expense of traveling to Houston continued to pile up, so I decided to look for doctors in the Dallas area whom I could see for the ongoing care of my heart checkups and pump refills. I was referred to the Baylor Heart Hospital. The cardiologist who would take over my care wanted to run additional tests, nothing new, the same old drill I had become accustomed to. The tests included an echocardiogram and a Holter monitor, followed by another tilt table test. The results confirmed everything we already knew, but the cardiologist wanted to ensure that things hadn't gotten any worse. After reviewing all of the results, he recommended a cardiac ablation, a procedure in which they would deliver energy in the form of heat to modify the tissues of the heart to try to correct the arrhythmia dysfunction.[11] The second option was to stay on the beta-blocker medication that I was currently on.

Over the next few weeks, I gave the matter more thought, and I decided to stay on the beta blockers and re-evaluate in another year. The procedure had its risks, and I didn't know if I wanted to cross that bridge just yet. While I still couldn't do things such as run or swim, the medication was allowing me, for the most part, to carry out my daily routine. I was gradually seeing progress compared to where I had started the journey with my heart issues.

By October, I was fully in the care of Dallas doctors. God had led me to a wonderful nurse practitioner under a pain-management doctor at the University of Texas Southwestern Medical Center to refill my pump on a regular basis and adjust the dosages. We seemed to hit it off well. She was very caring and made it a priority to ensure that I got off the oral baclofen (muscle relaxer) I was still taking and to set the dosage in my pump properly so that it would work at the level it was designed to work. Previously, with my trips back to Houston, it was difficult to set the medication to the proper dosage because there was always a risk that it would be set too high and I wouldn't make it back there as quickly as I needed to for an adjustment. Now that my care was in Dallas, the nurse practitioner and I spent some time getting the dosage in my pump to the level that was needed for me to be able to come off all medication except for my heart medicine.

Work seemed to be going well. I really enjoyed the role that I held and was continuing to grow in my responsibilities and gain the trust of senior leadership. Before long, I was promoted to a higher position.

Throughout the winter and into the spring, I developed strep throat repeatedly. Every time I finished a round of antibiotics and got better, I was soon right back where I started. I knew that I had a lot on me and was constantly pushing myself to maintain all that was on my plate, which didn't help the situation.

By mid-April, I seemed to be either in my doctor's office or at an urgent-care facility every few weeks. The final straw came in May when my throat swelled to the point where doctors were concerned that it would become too inflamed and cause difficulty breathing. I was referred to an ENT (an ear, nose, and throat surgeon).

After one look at all my records and my throat, the surgeon stated, "David, your tonsils need to come out. I recommend that we do it here soon. Based on the number of antibiotics you have been on over the last few years, there will soon come a point where they won't work, and you'll have another set of problems."

I agreed to move forward even though I was dreading another surgery. I just couldn't catch a breath, constantly moving from one thing to another. Ever since I had shifted to night classes, the program was year-round. I only had a short break in the summer, so I scheduled it for then.

Before I knew it, I was in another hospital, and another operation was about to begin. I signed the forms and was wheeled off to surgery.

Recovery didn't take as long as with some of the major

surgeries I'd previously had. It was only a couple of weeks before I was back into my normal routine, prepared to finish off the last few months of my senior year.

CHAPTER EIGHTEEN

An Unexpected Turn

Not only so, but we also glory in our sufferings, because we know that suffering produces perseverance; perseverance, character; and character, hope.
—Romans 5:3–4 (NIV)

The big week had arrived. College graduation was only a few days away. I had worked so hard over the last four-and-a-half years for the moment when I could hold that diploma in my hands. I had overcome so many different obstacles and was proud that all of the hard work, the countless long hours, and the frustration of keeping up with so many moving pieces was paying off.

My family members started making their way to Dallas. Some came by plane while others decided to drive and make it a memorable, scenic trip to Texas, stopping at various cities along the way. I was blessed to have several family members present in Dallas with me to celebrate this special milestone in my life.

Friday, May 9, 2008 arrived! We had beautiful weather for graduation day. The temperatures were in the mid-eighties, and the sun shone brightly as all of the graduates stepped into the large megachurch building where the graduation ceremony was being held. Since I had shifted to night classes halfway through my college program to align my class schedule better with my doctor appointments and work schedule, I hadn't seen some of my fellow classmates in over a year. I could see the excitement written on everyone's faces. I had thought of this day many times, picturing what it might look like.

The ceremony began, and one by one, each college graduate walked up on stage to receive his or her diploma. When my name was called, I heard a large cheer fill the room. I walked up to the stage and shook hands with the president of the college while I held my diploma in my other hand. As I looked out across all the people, I felt immense gratitude.

When I had first moved down to Dallas five years before, I had questioned if I could make it. I had determined in my mind that I was going to finish despite the obstacles I would face. No one, except maybe my family, knew just how hard this journey had been on me. There had been so many times when I hadn't felt at all good physically, but I had forced myself to keep studying. My days were typically twice as long as other students' because I often had to stay up to the wee hours of the morning to make up for time that I had spent at a doctor's appointment, enduring a procedure, or working to help make ends meet. My calendar was full of flights, hotel reservations, work, and class schedules. All of this hard effort and time that I put into the degree made me appreciate and value the diploma even more.

Toward the end of the graduation, they had a few awards to hand out. One of these was the Lucille Perkins award, given to the student who exemplified academic excellence, Christian character, and service. The facilitator announced, "And the award goes to—David Rose!"

I was blown away. Academically, I knew that I had worked hard to maintain my school grades, but to be viewed by fellow classmates and professors as demonstrating outstanding Christian character and community service put a smile on my face. I hadn't realized just how much my persistent will to live, my determination to maintain a good attitude through this challenging journey, and my decision to take something that was meant to harm me and turn it into something good had impacted and inspired so many people around me. I was truly honored and blessed by such a kind gesture.

As my family departed that weekend to head back to Ohio, I thanked them and told them how much it meant to me for each of them to be present to celebrate this big milestone in my life.

Four Weeks Later

My family and I had planned to go on a vacation a month after graduation. We had spent the last few years being pulled in different directions during my recovery process, and we'd had little time simply to hang out as a family with no actual agenda.

Since I worked in the corporate office of a major hotel company, I had searched earlier in the year for a place where we could all get away for a while. I ultimately was able to secure a week at a beach resort in Waikoloa. With all the airline miles that both my mom and I had accrued over the last few years while traveling from one city to another, we had enough points to cover our entire trip. Therefore, we only had our food expenses to cover during our week on the Big Island. I believe that it was God's way of saying, "Well done! Thank you for being the light to those around you over the past few difficult years."

My family and I set out on the adventure. When we arrived at the resort after a long day of travel, we had the option to take a boat ride (similar to the River Walk boat ride experience in San Antonio) that would take us down a canal to our room, or we could take a train. I had never stayed at such a large resort before, and I was mesmerized by all that it had to offer.

One of the experiences we had was going out for a dinner boat cruise. I had the privilege while in high school to do something similar, and I highly recommended it to our family. I didn't know until we had purchased the tickets and were actually boarding the boat that it was more of a sailboat than a larger ship like I had experienced in Florida. Needless to say, the experience was not as delightful as we thought it would be. Several of my family members, including myself, felt completely nauseous from the rocking of the boat out at sea all afternoon. But that is what makes an adventure an adventure. You never know until you try something. My family and I look back on it and laugh at this experience now, though at the time, none of us were laughing!

During my downtime one day on the beach, I stopped and reflected on the last couple of years and what I had learned. I realized at that moment that seasons come and go. At times, it seems like a particular season will never end. The last few years had been the most difficult period of my life. So often, I wanted to know the course of treatment right away and have a clear path to relief of my symptoms, but that just wasn't the case.

As a young man, I had a sense of urgency and wanted things to happen quickly. I didn't like to pause and wait. Who does? I soon learned the true meaning of patience. Over those difficult years full of uncertainty and obstacles, God taught me how to persevere and keep fighting through my suffering, and He taught me how to be a better person in general. He taught me at a young age what was truly important.

When I set out for Dallas after graduating from high school, a part of me was running from past hurts and the frustration that had built up within me. I knew that I still needed to work through those feelings, but I was grateful that I had at least started to open up my lower compartment. In my early teen years, I had focused mostly on myself, but the experience of the accident and everything that had followed had taught me how to love other people and had redirected my priorities in life. God had blessed me in so many ways. Now that I had graduated from college, I was looking forward to all that the future had in store for me, including the opportunity to slow down some and begin the healing process.

Throughout that week in Hawaii, I made many great memories with my family. It was good simply to experience the peacefulness of the waves hitting the rocks, laughing as a family again, and enjoying each other's company. This was something that we all needed. I didn't know at the time that this vacation together was giving us unity and peace before the next storm that lay ahead of us.

We all said our goodbyes on Saturday evening and departed from Kona International Airport on overnight flights back home. When I landed Sunday morning, I called my parents and sister to ensure that they had made it back safely.

On Monday morning, I was up early to head into work at the corporate office. I had been out for a little over a week, so I spent the next couple of days catching up with emails, meetings, and the team I was managing before heading out again on Friday.

A good friend of mine, Abel, was getting married in San Antonio, so I had taken Friday off from work. I had a doctor's appointment to refill my pump prior to heading to the airport to catch a flight. The rehearsal dinner would be that evening. When I left the University of Texas Southwestern hospital in Dallas, I proceeded onto the I-35 highway. I was moving along with traffic until suddenly the person directly in front of me had a tire blowout. The driver of the vehicle was able to maintain control of the car. The driver slowed and drove to the shoulder area of the freeway. Fortunately, I was able to break. The person behind me, however, was not, and he plowed directly into the back end of my car. As I heard the sound of our vehicles colliding, disappointment and fear surged through me, and I thought, *"I can't believe this is happening again!"* I had just wrapped up my injuries from the previous car accident. I said a quick prayer, hoping that the sudden jolt wouldn't cause any of my previous injuries to reset.

Police arrived and took down our statements and insurance information. I instantly felt discomfort in my neck area and a tingling sensation down my arm, but when the police officer asked if I needed to go to the hospital, I simply declined and said that I was fine. I knew the drill should any of the injuries reset. At least I knew whom I needed to contact.

Thankfully, the car was still drivable, so I headed on to the airport. I arrived in San Antonio later that afternoon and went straight to the rehearsal dinner. Throughout the evening and into the morning, the discomfort progressed, but I told myself that it was only whiplash from the collision.

Abel's big day arrived! I held my composure, being as supportive as ever for him, though inwardly I wasn't feeling so great. The tingling sensation felt like there was something crawling up and down my nerve, starting in the brainstem and moving down through the neck and into my shoulder area. My neck was tight and difficult to move, which was no surprise since whiplash typically causes soreness.

I carried on with my various roles as a groomsman

throughout the afternoon and into the late evening. I had learned over the years how to put my game face on and pretend that all was well despite knowing that something wasn't right with my body. After the newlywed couple departed, I helped to clean up the dining room hall before I called it an evening and headed back to the hotel.

The next day, I woke up to news that I wasn't prepared for. I looked in the mirror and saw that my right shoulder area had once again collapsed. I stood there in disbelief. It was as if my entire world had just stopped. My mind began to flutter with anguish and anxiety, thinking of how difficult the last journey was on my family and me. I couldn't imagine going through it all again. For a moment, it was as if a movie was playing in my mind. I thought back to the time when I had looked at my reflection in the glass door of the car in the parking lot of the physical therapy office, the first time I was made aware of my injury. Then my mental movie immediately flashed to the disappointment of multiple tests and doctors' office visits. Lastly, I thought of the critical surgery that I had gone through to have the nerve repaired.

Still staring at myself in the mirror, I picked up my phone and called my mom. She could hear the disappointment in my voice.

"Mom, my shoulder has dropped again."

"Are you serious?" she replied. I knew that she was in as much disbelief as I was and trying to process the information.

"Mom, by looking at it, I'm guessing that my shoulders are a good seven inches apart. Last time, it took almost two weeks before the shoulder dropped, and this time it has been less than forty-eight hours. I'm looking at my shoulders in the mirror, and it appears to be much worse than the previous time."

"I'm sorry, David," she replied.

Words couldn't make me feel better. I knew that we were both thinking, *"Here we go again."*

"Are you going to try and go to the hospital?" she asked.

"No, I will just wait and call Dr. Nath tomorrow. I know that there isn't anything the hospital can do but prescribe me medicine. I'm going to pack up my things and head to the airport here shortly. Where are you all now?"

"Texarkana," my mom replied.

"Well, you all be safe driving. I will call you when I land back in Dallas."

CHAPTER NINETEEN

The Ultimate Questions: *Why?*

Have I not commanded you? Be strong and courageous. Do not be afraid; do not be discouraged, for the LORD your God will be with you wherever you go.
                                                            —Joshua 1:9 *(NIV)*

When I touched back down at DFW Airport, my parents called and informed me that they were getting close to Dallas. They were relocating to the DFW area and were driving down from Ohio over the weekend. The factory where my Dad was working had started laying people off and was accepting early retirements. He had been there for a little over fifteen years and was more than ready for a change, so he accepted an early retirement package.

I picked up my car that I had parked at the airport and headed to my apartment. By the time I had arrived back home, my parents had just pulled into the apartment complex. They were planning to stay with me for a while until they got jobs, settled in, and found an area of the metroplex where they wanted to get a house. I had been living on my own for a few years now and had become accustomed to being independent since my family was so far away. It was going to be an adjustment having three of us under one roof, in an apartment no less, but I happily accommodated them, knowing that they would have done the same for me.

By Monday, three days after the accident, my entire thoracic area on the right side had weakened and dropped substantially lower than it had in the first occurrence back in October of 2003. My entire neck, my upper and middle back, and my shoulder area felt like the muscles were being stretched and pulled apart piece by piece as the weight of the collapsed scapula put a tremendous strain on them. I could feel the tingling sensation in my nerves that went up and down my neck area. I had a terrible ache in my right ear, as if I had an ear infection.

The sudden impact of the collision had also caused the muscles in my legs to get tighter and tighter, resulting in discomfort similar to an ongoing charley horse and making it more difficult to walk and to go down stairs. I had to increase my oral muscle relaxers until I could get an appointment with my infusion-pump specialist to adjust the dosage. I kept praying that my heart condition wouldn't go backward. Over the last year, the lightheadedness had subsided, and my inappropriate sinus tachycardia was being managed through medicine.

I contacted Dr. Nath on Monday morning to get advice and to fill him in on what had occurred over the weekend. He told me to work with an area doctor to have an MRI conducted and an EMG test completed prior to seeing him. As before, the EMG could not be conducted until three weeks had passed after the accident to ensure that the nerve wasn't still firing, which would give an inaccurate reading. In the meantime, I found a local doctor who ordered an MRI of the cervical spine. The test was conducted, and the scans came back normal, which I had expected. I followed up with my pump doctor, who substantially increased the medicine that was being transmitted intravenously into my spinal cord through the Medtronic infusion pump.

I found myself once again having to be patient. The waiting process was beginning all over again. *"God, did I not learn what I was supposed to from the first accident? Why is all of this happening again?"* I asked.

A little over three weeks after the accident, I was back in one of the doctor's offices having an EMG test conducted. I already knew inwardly what the test results would show, and I braced myself. Sure enough, after the doctor completed the test, he sat down and looked at me.

"David," he said, "your eleventh cranial nerve has been damaged. I recommend surgery, and I can refer you to a local neurosurgeon."

I thanked him and told him that I would be following up with my neurosurgeon in Houston who had operated on the nerve initially after the first occurrence to determine how he wanted to proceed.

On Wednesday, August 6, I boarded another Continental Airlines flight bound for Houston. As I was proceeding down the jet bridge, I thought about how many trips I had made down to Houston over the last few years. It was August, so I was prepared for temperatures to be well over one-hundred degrees. I was used to that from living in Dallas. It was the humidity that always seemed to hit me the most.

When I arrived, I picked up the car that I had rented for the day. I had booked a late return flight so I could be back at work the next day. As I sat in Dr. Nath's office later that afternoon, I couldn't believe that I was going through this all over again. I thought back to when I had sat in that exact lobby just over four years before. I was so young and ready for answers, yet nervous about what the future would hold. Years later, I sat there again, having already experienced a difficult journey. I somewhat knew what to expect, but that wasn't exactly comforting.

I met with Dr. Nath, and he evaluated the EMG report and my upper thoracic area. "David, based on your history," he said, "I recommend that we try the route of physical therapy first before operating."

I was okay with a conservative route. Dr. Nath mentioned that with me already having a previous surgery, if we could free up the nerve and allow it to heal itself, that would be the best outcome. The surgery had risks, even more now that I had scar tissue from a previous surgery. I thanked him for his time and headed back to the airport.

Over the next two months, I had anywhere from two to three physical therapy sessions per week before having the EMG repeated. In late September, the EMG test result showed that the nerve was no longer entrapped. However, I still had the winging of the scapula. We continued with the physical-therapy sessions to try to strengthen the muscles, hoping that the nerves would grow back in due time. On average, nerves typically grow back at a rate of one inch per month.

Unfortunately, with my entire right thoracic shoulder area being collapsed (a difference of twelve or more inches compared to my left side), the weight of the shoulder was putting a tremendous amount of strain on my mid- to lower back. My condition was only getting worse instead of improving as we had hoped. My right shoulder was getting stiff, so I had difficulty bringing my arm out very far from me. Daily I was losing more and more mobility in the arm, something that I hadn't experienced with the previous injury. Simple things such as shaving, brushing my hair, and eating became harder and harder since I was right-handed.

I had other ongoing symptoms that only seemed to worsen, including constant ear pain that intensified as the weather changed. My neurologist believed that the pain in my ear was related to nerve damage as well. I was on a cocktail of different medicines, all of which I tried to avoid if at all possible because the side effects prevented me from a majority of the activities that I needed to do each day. My muscles throughout my neck and shoulder area felt as though they had been stretched. They ached constantly. In addition, new symptoms arose that I had not experienced after the first car accident, including problems with my digestive system. After eating, I felt really bad, but I couldn't put my finger on a reason.

I would often read Joshua 1:9, which reminded me that I

was called to be strong and courageous. The part about not being discouraged was hard at times. I knew that God was with me and was helping me through this process, just like He had after the first accident. I was determined not to fall into the trap of feeling sorry for myself, but instead to keep moving forward while doing my best to maintain a positive attitude despite my circumstances. I didn't know at the time that the constant "go, go" mentality was part of a coping mechanism to avoid dealing with emotions related to my past experiences as well as everything I was going through in my current situation.

> Journal Entry (Sunday, October 5, 2008): I feel my independence slipping through my fingers day by day. The smallest and simplest things that I used to do are becoming so hard for me that I can no longer do them on my own. I'm bottling all of this inside because I don't know how to communicate how I truly feel deep inside to anyone. God, help me.

Toward the end of October, Dr. Nath's nurse called me and told me that he wanted to refer me to another surgeon to evaluate my case given that little to no progress had been made with physical therapy. I jotted down the information and called the surgeon, who was based at the University of Nebraska Medical Center. I spoke to the nurse and scheduled an appointment for Wednesday, November 19, a week prior to Thanksgiving.

While I was waiting for the appointment to come, days seemed to fly by. I was in the middle of our busiest time of the year at work. Managing a team and dealing with my health issues wasn't always easy, but somehow I kept going. Outside of work, I was still keeping up with all of the different moving pieces that it took to run a nonprofit organization. Sometimes I would debate whether To Give A Smile was something I should continue to do, but every time I thought about giving it up, someone or something would come along to inspire me to keep doing what I loved. I knew deep down that we were making a difference in our community and around the world. This journey was teaching me additional patience, humility, and the motivation to keep the organization running through a difficult season.

"Now boarding all passengers for Omaha," a voice announced over the intercom at DFW International Airport. I took a late flight on Tuesday evening after work. The next morning, I sat in the waiting area of a new hospital, waiting to be called back. I didn't know what to expect or what the doctor would be like. I had dealt with so many doctors and surgeons over the years and had seen a good mixture of different personalities to say the very least.

The nurse announced my name, and I went back to the examining room. In walked Dr. Nystrom, an upper extremity and microvascular surgeon, who introduced himself and reached out to shake my hand. We conversed for a little while, beginning with small talk. He asked where I worked and where I was from before moving to the topic of my medical history.

Then Dr. Nystrom had me stand up and take off my shirt so he could begin the evaluation. He was surprised when he saw how severely off-balance my body was from the winging of the scapula. He scratched his head and said something along the lines of, "Dr. Nath thinks I can do something, does he?"

I had seen and heard so many reactions over the years that nothing really surprised me anymore. I simply smiled and replied, "Yep!"

"Well, we're going to give it the best shot we can," he said, smiling back at me.

I could already tell that Dr. Nystrom was going to be a good, caring doctor from his demeanor and the short interaction we'd had so far. He stepped out of the room and brought back a few different syringes. He went on to explain that the loss of movement in the arm and possibly the winging of the scapula could be results of internal pain trigger points. The idea was to inject numbing medicine up and down the shoulder and neck area to see if I regained movement. I have to admit that I was a little skeptical, but I thought, *"What do we have to lose?"*

He took the syringes and inserted the medicine throughout the upper extremity. We waited for a few minutes to allow the medicine to kick in, and then he asked me to try to move my arm. I did so and found that I was able to move my arm fully again, and the winging of the scapula improved significantly. I couldn't believe it! I stood there in denial for a few seconds. Then I smiled widely as I looked at myself in the mirror. Over the last few months, I had started to lose hope that my arm would be restored to how it was prior to the accident.

The medication only lasted for a brief few minutes before all of my symptoms returned, but I had a renewed sense of hope. Dr. Nystrom was amazed and excited that it had worked as well as it had.

He sat down with me, looked me in the eye, and said, "David, this is good news. You are a candidate for the surgery."

He went on to explain what the surgery would involve and walked me through what the recovery time would look like. The only big difference from my previous surgeries was that this one would require me to be fully awake throughout the procedure so I could communicate with him and the medical staff. He assured me that they would keep me as comfortable as possible throughout the surgery, but this was the best way to identify pain triggers and test the movement of my arm while in surgery. I thought it over and agreed to move forward.

As I flew back to Dallas that evening, I had hope that I would be able to regain some of the movement of my right arm, if not full movement.

One Month Later

The month of December arrived. It was always my favorite time of the year. This year, everything seemed to happen quickly. I was at the height of my busiest time of the year at work. My team and I were working long hours, trying to get numerous rates loaded for top accounts for our hotels all throughout the United States. Outside of work, I was getting prepared for another surgery.

The company I worked for had been sold a year earlier to an investment company. As part of the acquisition, the investment company was re-evaluating and aligning different departments to streamline support. There had been talk that either the office in Dallas, where I worked, or the Memphis location would be closed. By this time, the economy was not doing well. We were in the midst of a recession. I had determined that it would be best for me to fit in the surgery before the end of the year since my health insurance company had approved it and the future of my employment was unknown.

Surgery was scheduled for Monday, December 29. My family and I flew in the day prior and had a dinner of my choice, as was our tradition. I was as grateful as ever for my family's constant support.

Another big day arrived. It was the same drill as before: the check-in process, the insurance forms, the waivers, the surgery prep. Before long, I was saying goodbye to my family once again as I was wheeled back into the OR.

The setting was new to me. I was in a different hospital in a different city, and I would be completely awake through the entire surgery. The drugs necessary to keep me comfortable were inserted into my IV. The medical team got me all prepared once I was in the OR. I was placed in a surgical chair. I would be sitting up instead of lying flat this time. The surgeon thought it would be best given the current restrictions of my arm. The preparations for the surgery continued, including covering me up completely with the medical drapes and swabbing my entire brachial plexus area, my shoulder, and beneath my armpit with betadine. This was my first time being awake to observe all of the various steps taken before a surgery.

Soon the medicine kicked into gear. I didn't feel any pain as the medical team tested different trigger points before beginning the operation. The medicine caused me to become overly talkative, and I carried on a stream of conversations with the medical team.

Dr. Nystrom walked in and asked, "Are you ready, David?"

"Yes, I am," I replied.

They covered my right side so that I wouldn't be able to see what was going on surgically. I was very much aware of what was taking place, but it helped that I wasn't able to see all of the blood.

Surgery began. Dr. Nystrom and I conversed throughout the procedure. At different points, they would reduce the medicine so that I could identify old pain compared to new pain. During those times, I would also be asked to try different hand movements to see if we had made progress. Little by little, we were seeing results of more function in my arm. Dr. Nystrom asked me if I wanted to continue with the procedure, and I said, "Yes."

Time continued to pass. I was still carrying on conversations with the medical staff. I don't recall what exactly we talked about, but I'm sure it was anything that came to mind.

After a little over four hours in surgery, I was becoming a

little weak. Dr. Nystrom had me try to move my arm, and I did. To my amazement, I was able to move my arm fully again. I couldn't believe it! I didn't notice any restrictions, and the winging of the scapula had improved significantly. Dr. Nystrom was as stoked as I was!

After taking a series of different pictures on top of the film that was being recorded throughout the procedure, Dr. Nystrom asked me if I wanted to proceed into the neck area. I hadn't been able to bend my neck for some time since the accident. However, I had taken all that I thought I could endure. I was becoming extremely weak and nauseous, so I told him that we would need to stop.

Stitching came next, followed by bandaging. A good thirty minutes later, I was being wheeled back into the recovery room. *"I made it through another surgery,"* I thought before falling asleep.

I stayed in Omaha for a little over a week, recovering from the surgery. I had a follow-up appointment with Dr. Nystrom to check my incision and the movement of my arm. He was still stoked about the outcome of the procedure, and he told me how much he had learned from my case. He asked if I would be willing to give permission for my case to be used for medical articles and seminars. I gave my consent, thinking that if I could help anyone else through all of this, I would gladly do so.

CHAPTER TWENTY

The Will to Press On

...but one thing I do, forgetting those things which are behind and reaching forward to those things which are ahead, I press toward the goal for the prize of the upward call of God in Christ Jesus.
—Philippians 3:13–14 *(NKJV)*

By February, a little over two months had passed since my recent surgery. I was grateful to have movement back in my arm. The simplest things that I once had difficulty doing I was now able to do on my own again. I was so appreciative of and thankful for the progress that had been made.

My work situation, on the other hand, hadn't gotten any better. The entire department was on pins and needles, waiting to see whether we would keep our jobs. We had been informed that either the Dallas or the Memphis department would be cut. I knew that either way, the outcome would be difficult because one department would be taking on the other. I had created some great friendships over the years with my travels back and forth to Memphis, and I knew that the decision would impact everyone in both departments.

Toward the end of the month, the Memphis team was informed that their jobs would be cut and the Dallas team would be absorbing the operation over the course of the next three months. My team, along with the rest of the department, received the news later that afternoon from a member of the executive team. I was grateful to be keeping a job but saddened for everyone impacted in Memphis. The Dallas leadership team had to start working immediately on our transition plans to absorb the operation.

Days became longer and longer through the weeks ahead. I tried to think of everything that needed to be included in our transition while keeping the operation that we had in place going. Often I would end my day around 1 a.m., only to be back up at 4:30 a.m. to start all over again. My calendar was filled with back-to-back conference calls and multiple trips to Memphis.

When I thought that I couldn't take on anymore, my right thoracic area dropped once again, resulting in the scapula penetrating out further from the rib cage. I had followed all of the doctors' orders over the last few months and couldn't understand why this was happening again. I had recently returned to exercising and lifting weights for the first time since the accident, all of which I had been cleared to do. Thankfully, I still had full range of motion, so the recent surgery had still been worth it.

With all that I had going on, I worked in another trip to Omaha to see Dr. Nystrom. Once again, I was sitting in the waiting room, this time just staring at the wall until my name was called. I was exhausted, plain and simple.

Dr. Nystrom re-evaluated my back, shoulder, and right thoracic region and informed me that, unfortunately, there were times when patients require an additional, follow-up surgery. He said that he would proceed with putting the request into the insurance company.

In the meantime, I headed back to Dallas to continue with my day-to-day responsibilities of trying to absorb an entire operation. My original staff of eight team members became a team of fourteen members. The task wasn't easy, and it took a huge toll on me over those few months. By the end of May, the Dallas team had taken over the full operation. I was glad to see this challenge behind me.

Shortly after the consolidation of offices had been completed, I was off to Peru with a team to conduct our first medical mission trip. Over the last eight months, I had been maintaining all of the responsibilities of work, medical treatment, family time, and planning for this mission trip. I didn't know what to expect, but I was excited to get a break from Corporate America, my day-to-day responsibilities, and my health situation while seeing the dream of a medical mission that God had put on my heart a few years ago come into existence.

When we all arrived, we spent the rest of the day doing some sightseeing in Trujillo, Peru, before our medical mission efforts began. On Monday, the team assembled, gathered our supplies, and headed out to our first remote location.

As we pulled up to our first clinic site, I was surprised to see the number of families already lined up to see a doctor. I was later informed that families had begun the journey to our clinic as early as 4 a.m. Throughout the day, I saw people waiting patiently, without complaint, for hours upon hours to see a doctor. In that moment, I realized just how blessed I was. It seemed that every corner I turned in Dallas, there was a doctor's building, a hospital, or an urgent-care facility, while in this remote area of Peru, people would go years without seeing a doctor. I knew then that the medical missions would remain a focus of the organization as we moved forward.

When I arrived back home, I had received a letter in the mail from my medical insurance company denying the surgery with Dr. Nystrom. It was considered an elective procedure. I was back to square one again. Dr. Nystrom's office told me that they would submit additional paperwork to see if they would be able to sway the decision. Weeks went by without further updates.

A New Hope

Throughout the summer months, my condition remained about the same. My upper body was once again severely off-balance, with my shoulders about twelve inches off from each other, which resulted in a great amount of discomfort in my mid-back, neck, and thoracic area. I still had the ongoing ear pain, and the digestive issues also remained. After eating, I would often lie on the floor or in my bed, feeling terrible. I was anxious about eating since it seemed that everything I ate would put my body on a roller coaster. I never knew how it would respond.

The Rolodex filing folder where I kept the business card of every doctor I saw was becoming larger and larger. I had cardiothoracic surgeons, neurosurgeons, movement specialists, neurologists, microvascular surgeons, orthopedic surgeons, cardiologists, and most recently, a gastroenterologist. Trying to keep all of the doctors and appointments straight in my mind was a challenge.

I was referred to different specialists and surgeons in the Dallas area since the approval for the surgery never came through. With my upper body so severely off-balance, one of the doctors recommended a scapula fusion surgery, in which doctors would fuse the scapula to the rib cage. I considered the surgery for a short period but didn't believe that was a bridge I wanted to cross at this point in my life.

As the days continued to go by, I felt internally numb. I was going through the motions of the day, but I struggled with my thoughts. I often didn't feel well, and I wondered if this would be the new normal for me. While I believed that God could heal my physical body, I started to doubt whether I would see that day again as the odds were stacking up against me. Above all else, I struggled with my inner self and the past that still weighed heavily on my shoulders. Negative thoughts continued to float around my mind, including self-doubt, insecurities, and problems with relationships. The little things people would say sometimes pushed me over the edge. I maintained a calm demeanor but inwardly raged with frustration.

Over time, through a series of different tests, doctors were able to pinpoint the issues related to my digestive system and what was causing all of the internal chaos after eating. They informed me that I might have had an underlying condition that resulted in a sensitivity to various foods and the accident had caused things to kick into high gear. I was put on a stricter diet, and my digestive issues improved gradually.

Weeks turned into months with no further updates regarding my upper-extremity imbalance. My nurse practitioner encouraged me to see a local neurosurgeon there at the University of Texas Southwestern hospital, the place where I went regularly for my pump refills. My hope was fading, and I didn't expect much, but I thought, *"What could it hurt to see another doctor?"*

The local neurosurgeons assessed my case and highly recommended that I see another neurosurgeon down in Houston. I decided to give it one more shot. I scheduled an appointment for the beginning of October but found out days later that my grandfather had passed away back in Ohio. I adjusted the appointment to late October so I could fly up to be with my family for the funeral.

We gathered together as a family to pay our respects to my grandfather and the life he had lived, and I realized in that moment how short life truly is. Over the years, I had pretended to have it all together even though I was struggling inwardly. The past remained dormant while additional layers of pain and frustration piled on top of it. I was running. I hid behind work, the nonprofit, a full schedule, and travel just to stay busy. The busyness helped to take my mind off everything else going on.

As I stood there, looking around at my family, I reflected on the memories we had shared with my grandfather. I began to consider what I would want others to think of me and the life I had lived and the legacy I left behind. After that day, I thought deeply about the man I was and the man I wanted to become.

Days later, I sat in the waiting room of another medical building in Houston. I was called back and placed in one of the rooms. While I was waiting, I knelt down in the observation room and asked God to give the doctor wisdom and clarity, and I prayed for His will to be done. Shortly afterwards, Dr. Kim walked in and introduced himself. He looked at some of the medical reports that I had, along with another EMG test that had recently been done, and he recommended a surgery to repair and, if need be, a nerve graft to help stabilize the spinal accessory nerve, as it was once again entrapped. Due to the amount of trauma the nerve had experienced over the years, he didn't know how good the results would be, but he believed that it was the best option for me.

Over the next few days, I gave the surgery further thought and continued to pray about it. Life was different for me now. I was in my mid-twenties. I held higher roles and responsibilities and had a better understanding of the risks of the surgery and the potential impact if it didn't go as planned. In this time of careful consideration, God gave me peace, and I decided to proceed with the surgery. The surgery was approved by insurance and was scheduled for December 16.

The weeks leading up to the surgery went extremely fast. Trying to get work, the nonprofit organization, and my personal commitments all aligned, caught up, and covered before being off for a month or more was always a huge undertaking to say the least.

I arrived in Houston on the evening of Monday, December 14, 2009. I spent the majority of the following morning at St. Luke's Episcopal Hospital for my pre-surgery appointment, and my immediate family flew in later that day. As I sat in the pre-surgery area, I could hardly believe that I would be undergoing another operation. I had become accustomed to the questions the medical team would need to ask and the testing that would be done the day before. Still, though this would be my seventh surgery since 2004, I never got completely used to it.

The surgery day arrived. I was up at 4 a.m. to say my morning prayer before we all headed to the hospital to get me checked in. Mine was the first surgery of the day, so the process between my arrival and my being wheeled back to the OR went quickly. I remained strong for everyone as I said my normal goodbyes and "I love you" before the medical team took me on my way.

As I was placed on the operating table, I felt more nervous than I had before any other surgery. I looked up at the bright lights and said another quick prayer, asking God to protect me and to give the medical team wisdom and steady hands as they proceeded through the surgery. Then I drifted off to sleep.

I woke up in the recovery room of the hospital, this time bandaged all over my entire neck and thoracic region.

The recovery nurse started asking me several questions, as they always do.

"Can you tell me your name?"

"David Rose," I responded.

"David, can you move your toes for me?" I did.

She then asked me if I could feel her touching my legs and arms.

I replied, "Yes, I can." A sigh of relief swept through me.

My mom joined me in the recovery room shortly afterwards. Her presence and smile comforted me. She asked me how I felt, and I said, "I'm okay."

"How did the surgery go, and why am I covered in so many bandages?" I asked.

"Dr. Kim said that your surgery went well. The nerve was intact but encased in scar tissue. He wanted to follow the nerve all the way down to ensure that no further entrapment was present to allow the best hope of recovery. He informed us that due to how long the nerve had been injured, he didn't know how well it would regrow. He said that we should know more in the next few months."

After our brief conversation, I sat there and thought, *"I have done my part."* I believed that God would repair the nerve in His timing.

Over the course of the next two days at the hospital, my biggest complaint was how sore my throat was. I expressed my concern, and the doctors reassured me that it was related to the intubation. They had put a tube down my throat to make it easier to get air into my lungs during surgery.

On Friday morning, I was released from the hospital. My mom and I drove back to Dallas so I could be in my own bed for recovery.

Over the weekend, I continued to get weaker with every hour that passed. Every time I tried to swallow, I could barely stand the discomfort. I developed a low-grade fever, and I knew that something wasn't right.

Monday morning came around, and my lymph nodes were swollen and bulging out all over my neck area. I told my dad that I needed to get to the doctor's office as soon as possible. I put my arm around his neck, and he helped to lift me out of bed and support my body weight as we went to the car. When I arrived at the doctor's office, the medical staff helped me into a wheelchair and took me in.

The doctor did an exam, including taking my temperature, looking into my throat, and feeling my neck area. She told me that I had a serious infection and that she would call in several different medications and a strong round of antibiotics. She then looked at my dad and said, "If he gets any worse or is not feeling any better within twenty-four hours, take him to the emergency room." My dad nodded and thanked her.

Over the next twenty-four to forty-eight hours, I started to feel a little better. I was so weak that I could hardly sit up. Coming off a big operation and then having an infection set my recovery time back, I had eaten barely anything in several days.

Slowly, over time, my appetite started to come back, along

with my humor. Over the next two weeks, my strength began to return, and I was getting back to my normal self.

Journal Entry (Tuesday, Dec 29, 2009): Yesterday was my post-op visit in Houston for the spinal accessory nerve repair surgery. It was quite a long day, but it was amazing to see how things just seemed to fall into place, from the flights being on time, to God giving me the strength to get through the day, to getting an earlier flight back.

I had a long discussion today with the nurse practitioner, Careen, regarding the surgery. She walked me through the ops report. During surgery, they identified significant scarring around the nerve (no surprise since I had a previous surgery in the neck area back in 2004), and they saw that a nerve tumor had developed (neuroma). The nerve was carefully dissected and freed up in surgery. A nerve conduction test revealed some signal, which was a good sign. The doctor stated that it could take up to two years before I see results. With the nerve being blocked for so long, there is a good chance it could be permanent; only time will tell. Lord, I know that whatever is meant to be will be. I just place it in Your hands.

As the days progressed, I started getting into a light routine as I prepared to go back to work. After a few weeks, I was back at my job. Corporate America hadn't changed much. In fact, it was becoming even more demanding since the recession hit, so I was glad that I had taken the time to recover before heading back to my day job.

It took me a couple of weeks to get caught up and back into my full work routine. The environment around me at work had changed and was continuing to evolve, with more responsibilities being added to everyone's plate. The company continued restructuring. Our department leadership team was always having meetings with consultants who came in to walk through what we did, the level of support we provided, ways we could automate tasks, et cetera. The thought always lingered in the back of my mind: *"Will I continue to keep my job, or will our department eventually be outsourced?"* Either way, I knew that it was out of my hands, so I just kept doing my best.

Outside of work, the financial toll of trying to pay all of the travel-related expenses and the medical bills that were continuing to pile up on top of my living expenses became overwhelming. Everywhere I turned, it seemed that every part of my life was in chaos.

In March, I was back in Dr. Kim's office for my three-month follow-up appointment. The right thoracic shoulder had improved slightly, which was a good sign. Dr. Kim reminded me that it would take time. Hopefully, the nerve would grow back at a rate of around one inch per month. Based on how long the nerve was, it could take anywhere from a few months to a few years to grow back fully. I continued to believe that one day, I would look in the mirror and see my upper body fully restored and back to normal.

By mid-summer, I had started to make preparations for my next surgery, replacement of the intrathecal infusion pump, which I had to have done every five to six years. It was hard to believe that it had already been five years since the operation I had endured to insert this device. It seemed like I had bounced from one doctor to another and one hospital to another over these past few years. I barely had time to catch my breath for a moment before having to prepare to go through the next surgery. My body barely had time to recover between operations. However, I could see the light at the end of the tunnel, as this would hopefully be my last surgery for a while.

October 12, 2010, came quickly. I was now in the care of another neurosurgeon for this surgery. I was grateful to be in Dallas this time instead of having to travel to some other city in the United States. During the pre-op appointment the previous day, I had recalled how hard this last surgery had been on me when I first went through the procedure. The medical team and neurosurgeon were all aware of the problems I had previously encountered and were going to take every precaution they could to prevent the spinal leak. Before I knew it, I was being wheeled back to the OR, and round eight began.

After the surgery, my bed was ordered to stay flat for twenty-four hours. The neurosurgeon also conducted a blood patch while in surgery in hopes of preventing a spinal leak. Blood was taken and injected into the location where the catheter was placed so it would clot and help to seal the spinal leak.

Things were going well post-surgery, and I was released from the hospital two days later. Recovery took much longer than anticipated. Even though the doctor had taken so many additional steps to help prevent the spinal leak from occurring, I still endured intense headaches and couldn't sit up for more than a few minutes at a time. Whenever I lay back down, the headache would subside.

The first week came and went with me lying on the couch, only getting up to use the restroom and grab some food, which I would take back to the couch to eat. The second week passed, and there was no change. I was getting tired of just lying around, watching movies. I called the nurse to see what the neurosurgeon thought, and we considered conducting another blood patch to try to seal the leak. However, the blood patch had its own risks. We agreed to give it another week and then re-evaluate.

The days went by slowly. I had always been an active individual, so lying completely flat came hard to me. While the downtime had been nice, it was starting to lose its attractiveness to say the very least. Toward the end of the week, though I still had headaches, I was starting to be able to tolerate sitting up for a little while, which was a great sign. The doctor and I agreed to hold off with the blood patch since I was making progress. It was just going to take time. Once again, my heavenly Father was reminding me of the importance of patience, and I began asking Him to direct me regarding what I should focus my thoughts on during this time.

My world prior to the surgery had been a whirlwind of constant activity and a packed schedule. The downtime began to renew a sense of purpose in me as I lay or sat there with no agenda and no commitments, just listening to God and dreaming about what He had in store for me. I reflected on the many times I had wanted to give up on life, my health, and healing from my dark past. However, through it all,

God's unending grace and love and His continual guidance had kept the spirit of pressing forward at the forefront of my mind.

During this season of pause, God began to lay upon my heart that I needed to forgive my abuser. In order to release my past and move on, I needed to take this essential step. I needed to do it for myself. I didn't know what forgiveness would look like in this case. I felt that I had moved on, but deep down, I was still hurt and frustrated about what had happened to me. I prayed to God to give me the courage and strength to confront my abuser. I was able to find him on Facebook Messenger, and I sent him a private message that I wanted to see him if he would be willing to meet up. He responded quickly and said that he would; I just needed to name the day and place.

CHAPTER TWENTY-ONE

Overcoming the Past

The thief comes only to steal and kill and destroy; I have come that they may have life, and have it to the full.
                                            —*John 10:10 (NIV)*

By mid-January, more than five weeks had passed since I had taken off for the surgery. I returned to work toward the latter part of our busy season. I had given my body the time it needed, and I felt good considering all that I had been through.

Less than a week after my return, my boss pulled me into her office and informed me that my role would be expanding and I would be responsible for globalizing different support processes. With this new change, I would be taking on a team in Glasgow, Scotland, that would start reporting to me. It would require a good amount of international travel, and my direct report would be increased to eighteen team members. During this time, the economy wasn't doing well. I didn't have any time to look for another job, and I knew that I still needed the health insurance. The new role came with no additional compensation or title change.

Knowing that the year ahead of me was going to be just as busy as any prior years, if not more so, I informed my boss that I needed to return home to take care of something in the early part of February. I knew that all of these directives for consolidating offices and globalizing support structures were not coming from her, but from the executive committee. She was given a task to do, and I understood that. I always respected her for not being quick to write me off. I'd had one surgery after another and knew that she could have found a way to get rid of me if she had wanted to. She always supported me and the rest of the leadership team and encouraged us to take any days off we needed to take care of personal things, never once asking for any additional information.

I booked my airline ticket and flew back to Ohio. Since my parents had moved to Texas, I hadn't been home in a while. My brother and his family would typically come down to see us. The closer I got to arriving in Fort Wayne, the more I ached inside. I felt sick in the pit of my stomach. I would rather have done just about anything else than confront my abuser. He had hurt me deeply, and I didn't know how the conversation would go.

The next morning, as I sat in the parking lot of the location where we planned to meet, I called a pastor friend of mine who had been a true gift to me. I had opened up to him and shared some of my past hurts. As we conversed, he encouraged me and told me that there would be a breakthrough and a release in my life after this conversation. He reassured me that he was praying for me.

I got out of the car, my stomach still churning. With every step I took, I prayed with intensity, asking God to give me the words to say and the strength and courage to address this man who had hurt me so profoundly.

I entered the building and saw standing in front of me the person who had so greatly impacted my childhood. I hadn't seen him since I had moved away from Defiance eight years before.

We sat down, and before I could get a word out, he said, "David, thank you for reaching out to me to meet up. I want you to know how sorry I am. There is not a day that goes by that I don't think about what I did and how I hurt you. I'm sorry, David."

I looked at him and said, "There are some things I need to get off my chest." I pulled out a letter I had written and began to read it to him:

Over the years, I have been challenged in more ways than I could ever have imagined. Before the car accident took place in 2003, I had buried the pain, the emotions, the frustration you had caused me.

I intended to continue carrying the excessive baggage of my past, planning not to tell a soul. I didn't want to feel defeated or less of a man by telling someone what had happened to me. I had the intention of never looking back.

With the emotional distress of the events that took place surrounding the accident, I neared a breaking point, and I couldn't move forward with the weight of the past on

my shoulders. Inside I was screaming for help. I felt like
I was about to suffocate.

I was full of questions that didn't have answers. My heart
was numb, and my life felt fake. Every day, I feared that
the past would seep out and become visible to others'
eyes. I finally reached my breaking point and threw up
my hands.

I'm alive, I'm here, and God has placed extraordinary
people in my life to help me overcome the pain and
suffering you have caused. A deep wound that I thought
would never be healed is slowly becoming a scar, a scar
that no longer aches like it once did. This scar is
becoming less and less visible; however, it still tells of a
past that I am no longer ashamed of or unwilling to speak
of.

I went on to share how the abuse had affected me,
including how I felt ashamed, guilty, and fake, how I
mistrusted other men, and how I had difficulty with
relationships. I told him how frustrated I had been deep
inside. I also shared how the abuse had made me a stronger
person, a protective person, and had given me a desire to
prevent similar things from happening to others.

I continued reading the letter I had written:

I want you to know that I'm not going to allow the past to
define me, but rather encourage me to change the world
and make it a better place.

With that said, when I was in Denver, Colorado, in the
summer between my sophomore and junior years of
high school, God called me to be a motivational speaker.
At the time, I had no idea why anyone would want to
listen to me. But now, reflecting on my life, I know I can

testify that no matter how many times life knocks me down, it is all about getting back up. My testimony is one of perseverance and hope.

In the years to come, I plan to speak out and talk about the abuse and the trials I have faced throughout my life, shedding some light and encouraging others who have been through similar trials never to give up.

I forgive you, and I pray that you are able to forgive yourself and move forward.

After I finished, a sense of release came over me.

"David," he said, "I'm truly sorry. Thank you for reaching out and forgiving me."

We conversed for a little while before I left. As I walked out of the building, I lifted my hands in victory. I felt the biggest weight being lifted off my shoulders! It had taken years to have this conversation, and I was so glad that I'd had the courage to do so. *"I'm an overcomer!"* I thought. *"God, have Your way in my life. Take and use my story as You would like."*

I spent the rest of the weekend hanging out with my brother, my sister-in-law, and my nephew. It was good to enjoy some time together since I didn't get to see them as much as I wanted.

On Monday morning, I flew back home. I was back for only a couple of days before I had to head out on my first trip to Glasgow, Scotland.

I stayed in Glasgow for two weeks, learning more about their processes and system limitations while getting to know each of the team members who would now be reporting to me. I tried hard to digest all of the information coming at me each day, and I spent my evenings getting caught up on emails from my team in Dallas. It felt like I was going back ten years or more in history due to how manual their processes were. It wasn't that they didn't want to advance, but the opportunity didn't always exist. Feeling overwhelmed, I wondered how I would manage to streamline support and bring this newly absorbed team up to the level they needed to be in order to mirror the operation in Dallas.

In order to clear my head and take my mind off the huge task I had been given, I decided to squeeze some sightseeing into my schedule over the weekend. I toured all throughout Scotland, taking an all-day land tour with three colleagues who had accompanied me on this trip. I always did my best to seize every opportunity to learn more about different cultures, as I never knew if or how many times I would be back to a certain location.

In the coming week, I wrapped up things there in Scotland before heading back to Dallas. Once again, I was only home for a short period. On top of being tasked to globalize the support process, I also had to sit on a committee panel that would be responsible for redefining the global process and the system that would be utilized in the future for processing rate loading, which required travel to these important meetings. I was off to London for a week, then home for two weeks, then back to Scotland for another two weeks. This type of travel schedule was becoming the new norm for me.

My calendar was being filled with both domestic and

international trips, and the days seemed to get longer and longer. I had always been fascinated with travel, and at first, it was exciting to see new places, but soon the glimmer wore off. I had no time for anyone, and what little time I did have I spent trying hard to keep the organization afloat.

On top of my day-to-day routine, part of my team was made up of contractors, so I never knew if they were going to show up to work. The line of business that I was responsible for wasn't something simple to train team members to do. I literally had to rethink the operation. I had my contractors start the process of various tasks, and then I had my more experienced, full-time team members complete them. This allowed them the chance to use their expertise to check the contractors' work for quality and, hopefully, catch any errors before the task was completed. Given the expanded role, my team was now responsible for processing over a million transactions a year, with more than sixty percent of those transactions during the fourth quarter. One simple mistake could cost anywhere from a few thousand to hundreds of thousands of dollars in lost revenue.

Overall, the morale of the team and the company, for that matter, was low. Who could blame them? I tried to do what I could to encourage the group, but with as many direct reports as I had and no buffer of additional support between me and the group I managed, such as a team lead, I couldn't keep up. I was constantly putting out fires, running from one meeting to another, and trying hard to keep up with emails, not to mention the ongoing travel.

There were so many days when I just wanted to throw up

my hands and walk out, but I knew that wasn't reality. I was becoming so burned out. Often it seemed like I bounced from one big obstacle in my life to another.

Before I knew it, 2011 was coming to a close. At the end of each year, I always enjoyed taking the time to reflect on what I had accomplished, memories that were made, and goals that were met while also taking a hard look at who I was and areas where I wanted to see change. This helped me to set the stage for what I wanted to focus on in the new year ahead.

I realized that this was my first full year since my first accident in 2003 that I didn't have one or two surgeries within a given year. The last seven years had, at times, seemed to be a blur, and this past year had been similar due to the demands of my job. I recognized just how much of my time I had been giving to my job. I worked nearly 24/7. With the consolidation and globalizing efforts, the high expectations, and my health problems, I felt numb and tired. I felt like a dripping faucet. I was functioning, but I wasn't nearly at my best.

While reading the book *The Circle Maker*, I came across a section that really jumped out at me: "Do the best you can with what you have where you are. Success is not circumstantial. We usually focus on what we're doing or where we're going, but God's primary concern is who we're becoming in the process."[12]

As I thought on that, I reminded myself that God had placed me in this current role and allowed me to endure so many health obstacles and other challenges in my life for a reason. He knew how exhausted and frustrated I was and

202

how desperately I wanted a change for my life. I decided that despite all the emotions I was experiencing, I would continue to keep the best attitude through this season until a new door opened.

A New Year's resolution that I set was to find a new job that would allow me more time to pause and catch my breath so I could begin the process of healing from all that I had endured over the past twenty-seven years of my life.

Two Months Later

I sat in the restaurant at my downtown hotel in Glasgow, Scotland. I had lost count of the number of trips I had made across the Atlantic Ocean, traveling either to a meeting or to visit my team in Glasgow. I had determined at the beginning of this year that a priority in my life would be taking a step down from the demanding life I was leading to reset and heal. An overwhelming peace came over me, and God confirmed in my spirit that this would be the last time I would be visiting the team there in Glasgow.

When I returned to Dallas, I continued to pray for guidance. I decided to accept a job with the same company but in a different department. I would have less responsibility in this new role. In most people's minds, it would be a step down.

In the weeks ahead, I felt like a huge weight had been lifted from my shoulders, but at the same time, I became depressed. The enemy started to fill my mind with doubts. Did I make the right choice? In my mind, I again heard that familiar refrain: *"David, you'll never amount to anything."*

Inwardly, I officially hit rock bottom. All of the constant running, either by choice or necessity, had taken a toll on me. I became determined to grow in my walk with the Lord and to process my past.

With fewer work responsibilities and minimal travel, I instead filled my afternoons with prayer and devotions. I often spent time in a secluded area by a river, where I could be away from the world. There I would journal, read God's Word, and process my thoughts. During this time, I rededicated my life to Him. I surrendered to God my family, my future family, my career, To Give A Smile, and speaking opportunities to come. I gave Him control to do what He wanted to do with my life. Through that season of prayer, I defined what success meant to me and wrote it down so that it would be a visual reminder every day and I wouldn't get caught up in things that didn't truly matter to me.

In the months ahead, I started, with the help of a Christian counselor, slowly peeling back and processing the layers of my past. We talked through my hurts and frustrations as well as the coping mechanisms I had developed over the years.

I would often land on the story of Joseph in the Bible and how he overcame so much. He was betrayed by his own brothers, sold into slavery, and falsely accused of trying to make a pass at a woman, which resulted in him being thrown into prison. I wondered what went through Joseph's mind. Was he frustrated? Did he wonder why one obstacle after another occurred, with no real break between them?

I admired Joseph's determination to keep a good attitude,

and I saw how God showed favor upon his life in the midst of the difficult seasons he was walking through. I could relate. While I was hurt by some of the things that had happened to me as a child, I still saw God's favor upon my life over the years. He allowed me to live when I was born. He prevented harm to my body when I fell from the bleachers. He saved me from both car accidents and brought the right physicians into my life to help with the healing. All along the way, God had always provided for my needs.

Just like Joseph, I was faced with a decision. When his brothers came to ask for food from him during a season of lack across the land, they did not know that it was Joseph to whom they were coming. When Joseph saw them, he had a choice either to hold on to the frustration and bitterness or to forgive his brothers. Ultimately, Joseph chose to forgive. As I read that, I recognized that I had made steps forward by forgiving my abuser, but I realized that there were other people in my life whom I still needed to forgive.

Determined to deal properly with my past, I set out to forgive those who had hurt me, including those who verbally bullied me and the person who had changed my life so much back in October of 2003 when he or she chose to keep driving despite not knowing my condition. While I didn't know the driver's name or story, I chose to forgive him or her in my heart, hoping that someday I would be able to do so face to face.

CHAPTER TWENTY-TWO

The Power of Giving

And we know that in all things God works for the good of those who love him, who have been called according to his purpose.

—Romans 8:28 *(NIV)*

In the months ahead, I started to realize how much more joy I had in my life. I was no longer bound in chains, retracing my past, but instead pressing forward with a mission. I started seeing things in a different light. I saw how God had orchestrated my steps, bringing the right people into my life at the right time. I was determined not to allow the past to define me, but rather to let it inspire me to change the world.

God had given me a story. It was ultimately His story, but He had chosen me to live it out. I realized that without going through a difficult season, it is easy to say how we're supposed to live. However, actually living out my trust in God and believing that He has my life in His hands when times get tough is completely different.

My fear, which was rooted in pride, kept me from seeking help from other sources in my life to enable me to let out all of the pain inside. Over the years, I had pushed and made excuses because I didn't know how to cope with the pain. I thought that telling someone what had happened would make everything better. For a small glimpse of a second, it felt like it did. It felt good to get it off my chest. However, at the end of the day, the pain was still there.

Through this period of pause and reset, I was dealing with the golf balls in my bottle, as I had seen illustrated at the youth conference in Denver, Colorado, back when I was sixteen years old. So many times, I had wanted to release the past, but I didn't really know how, nor did I seem to have the time to do so. I had bounced from one trauma to another since I graduated high school.

As I reflected on the last few years since my graduation from college, I realized that I was chasing after the wrong definition of success. I was getting carried away with the things of this world that didn't really matter to me and pawning off my God-given dream to be a motivational speaker and to grow To Give A Smile.

I began to view my past as something that I wouldn't change because I was seeing Him use it in a greater way. I recognized that there were opportunities I wouldn't have had if it hadn't been for the years and years of hardships.

One of the circled scriptures that I continued to hold in my heart as I pressed through this journey was Romans 8:28 (NIV):

And we know that in all things God works for the good of those who love him, who have been called according to his purpose.

The abuse, the years in and out of hospitals, the letdowns, the pain, and the suffering—all of this He was ultimately going to use. It amazed me how God aligned my steps. Sometimes I had wished that it was as simple as being hospitalized and completing all of the surgeries at once versus having to bounce from one doctor to another, with years of uncertainty, closed doors, and frustration. However, God had a purpose for the years of trials, and I saw how His hands were weaving it all together. He gave me encouragement right when I needed it, led me to the doctors I needed to see, and enabled me to come out stronger and more grateful for life.

In July of 2017, I received my final clearance from Dr. Kim, as my shoulders had aligned back to normal position. In addition, over time, my heart condition had completely reversed itself, and I could wean off the beta-blockers. As a result, I was able to return to most activities. It amazed me just how far I had come over the years.

Ever since the day I resigned from the previous position that I held and took the time to pause, rest, and deal with my past, I started to see God expanding To Give A Smile. At times, I would think that maybe I had started the organization at the wrong period of my life, but looking back, I can see that it was exactly the right time. So often, I wanted to give up. At times, I would lie on the floor of my bedroom or in a hospital bed, just praying for God to take my life. Each time, God laid on my heart the need to keep going, to persevere, because somehow He was going to use the pain and the trials for His glory.

To Give A Smile continued to grow, adding additional chapters in different cities throughout the United States, each one partnering with all of the children's hospitals and Ronald McDonald Houses in the area to host fun and uplifting activities to take children's minds off their current treatment. The events ranged from big toy drives to craft hours to atrium events to themed dinner nights at Ronald McDonald Houses for the kids and their families.

Through the years, I have met some amazing kids, and I want to share two examples of lives that have been impacted through our local outreach efforts.

There was an eight-year-old boy with stage IV cancer who was living in a hospital. His parents no longer had anything to do with him. This young boy's presence would light up a room. No matter how bad he felt, he continued to smile. Through our outreach events, we managed, for a moment, to take his mind off all that he was going through and give him the chance to be a kid and to laugh. Less than a year after we met him, he passed away. I like to think that, at least for a period of time, we took his mind away from the day-to-day treatment, gave him the chance to interact with people outside of the nurses and doctors he saw, and allowed him to dream.

There's also the story of Norah Sedars. In February of 2017, the Sedars family was staying at the Ronald McDonald House of Dallas while their daughter, Norah, was recovering from her eighth surgery. Norah had just been released from the hospital when our paths crossed. She was in a lot of pain, had extreme swelling, and was having trouble with the way she saw herself in the mirror.

That evening, To Give A Smile was hosting one of our Give Love Valentine's-themed outreach events. We prepared and served a hot meal to the families staying at the home, followed by an evening activity. Norah and her family were able to take part in the events. Toward the end of the activity, Norah walked up to the To Give A Smile volunteers and handed them a Valentine's Day card that she had made. All of the volunteers showed their appreciation. They were engaged, fully present, and made her feel like she was the only one in the room. Norah was grinning from ear to ear.

Deb, Norah's mother, later shared how that evening had touched her heart:

> As a mother, it is a shot in the heart to hear and see your daughter struggle with the way she sees herself and to know that there is nothing you can do to take away the pain she is experiencing. As parents, we fight so hard for a smile. But look at this picture. That is the impact you make! You warm a mama's heart when she sees her hurting daughter smile. When you serve a meal, talk with the families, play with kids, or even just refill their drinks, it helps, it heals, it shows love when that might have been the only time they felt it all day. Everything you all do makes a difference. You help families get through one more day. Thank you for sacrificing your time to show families love.

I know that through this journey, I have inspired others, but more often than not, these children whom I come across inspire me and my wonderful team to keep pressing forward.

Internationally, we expanded to sending medical mission teams to multiple countries around the world each year. At each location, the organization funded the entire mission, including medication, set-up fees, and staffing, never once requesting any payment in return from the thousands of people who have received life-saving medical treatment.

In 2009, we set out to begin our medical mission work, and in the fall of 2019, we celebrated over ten years of international outreach efforts. I will never forget seeing a young boy being carried into one of our medical mission clinics by his father. The boy was alive, but barely. He lay motionless. Doctors began the necessary treatment, and two days later, the boy walked out with life again.

This is one of many stories of children who are days or even hours away from death, more often than not due to simple things that we in the United States consider to be treatable with immunizations, food, or over-the-counter medicines. In third-world conditions, many families lack the resources to provide their children with healthcare.

To Give A Smile has the vision to expand our reach domestically and open chapters all across the United States as we continue to encourage children who are walking through a difficult season and their families. Internationally, we have the goal to place mobile medical clinics in the locations we serve while creating the infrastructure to support year-round clinics.

If my life and my relationship with God had taken a different path in my years as a child and a young adult, I don't know that I would have had the vision or the passion to carry out the long hours it takes to run a nonprofit, let alone the determination to keep pressing forward and building it despite lingering thoughts that I should give it up. Above all that, without the trials that I faced, I don't know that I would have the empathy to relate to the mothers I come across who are walking through some of the most difficult seasons in their lives. I probably wouldn't have the wisdom and perspective to look into children's eyes and tell them to hang in there even if no one has been able to give them an explanation for their condition. I wouldn't know that what young people who are being abused or called names need to hear most is that they are children of God and perfectly made in His image. My own years of constant obstacles have enabled me to relate to others who are suffering and to see how God's goodness is being carried out in the interactions I have with children and families who are walking through a difficult season.

I fully accept the calling to share the message of hope and to encourage people to keep pressing forward no matter what the journey brings. I don't know to what extent God is going to use my story through the speaking He laid upon my heart many years ago, but I look to the future, knowing that wherever I am, I am in a place where God can use me.

A quote commonly attributed to Eleanor Roosevelt says it well:

> Yesterday is history, tomorrow is a mystery, and today is a gift; that is why they call it the present.[13]

I could have died on October 24, 2003, but God kept me here, and now He is using my past for a greater purpose. I have been blessed with additional time, and I know that each day I have been given is worth living to the fullest.

God's Hope for You

I can do all things through Christ which strengtheneth me.
—Philippians 4:13 *(KJV)*

I hope that you have been encouraged through my story. Throughout my life, I have envisioned being in different places and achieving specific milestones by a certain age. However, I have come to realize as I have grown older that while I may try to plan my life, God ultimately directs my steps (Proverbs 16:9).

God's Word never promised us a life full of roses. In fact, Jesus told us that we would encounter trials and tribulations in this world. At the same time, He encouraged us to "be of good cheer" because He has "overcome the world" (John 16:33 NKJV).

I don't know what hardships and obstacles you have personally encountered, but I am a testament that God can take our most trying moments, our darkest days, and turn them into our greatest ministry. Our world needs people who will be transparent, not pretending that they have it all together, but instead being honest about what they're going through so they can heal and then help others who go through similar difficulties. Our world needs people who will persevere and stand for what is right so they can show others that there is hope.

One of my favorite movies is *Secretariat,* a true story about a remarkable horse and his owner, Penny Chenery.[14] Before the horse went on to make history, the owner was faced with a series of trials, and the odds were stacked against her.

Her father died before the prime of the horse's career, resulting in a significant inheritance tax that the family had to pay. Instead of caving in to the pressure from others, including her family, to sell Secretariat to meet the financial burden on the family, she decided to stand firm and walk by faith, trusting the instincts God had given her that this horse was special. Her response in the movie, which stood out in my mind and has encouraged me in various seasons, is:

> This is about life being ahead of you and you run at it! Because you never know how far you can go unless you run.

Despite all odds and the many trials that both horse and owner faced, Secretariat (also known as Big Red) won the Belmont Stakes by a record thirty-one lengths, which secured him the 1973 Triple Crown.[15] It's a remarkable story of being in a season in which it looks like there's little hope, but with faith and perseverance, that difficult time can lead to a great victory that, in turn, inspires other people.

I believe that we all have been placed on this earth for a purpose. God has given each of us unique gifts, talents, and dreams.

Life is short. I encourage you to release your past hurts in due time. We all cope and deal with our dark and trying moments differently. Don't rush the process, but lean into God to direct your steps toward healing.

Whatever happens, whatever you have been through, whatever you face in the future, choose to love with all of your heart. Dream like you have never dreamed before. Make the decision every day to press forward. Pray often and work hard. Pursue the calling and the dreams God has placed in your heart.

Go and run your race!

Acknowledgments

I am so grateful for the many people who have come alongside me, encouraging me, praying for me, and standing with me through various seasons and the trials that I have faced. I have been blessed in so many ways. An incredible community of people has helped me to get where I am today.

My heartfelt thanks goes out to all of the people who have brought their gifts and talents, their wisdom, insight, and passion to this book and helped to bring it into existence.

To my mother and father, Kelly and Gary, and my brother and sister, Daniel and Christina: Words cannot begin to express how much I appreciate you all. I am immmeasurably grateful for your love, support, and encouragement through the unexpected turns of life. You are God's gift to me.

To my Book Prayer team: Thank you all for taking the journey through this project with me. You all have been faithful with your encouragement and prayers through this season. Each of you has played such a pivotal role in my life, and I am grateful to be able to do life with you.

To my medical staff: Without each of you, I would not be

where I am today. Thank you for your many years of education and continual learning, for your dedication to your specialty, and for your heart to care for the sick even when it often means not seeing your own loved ones as much as you would like.

To the To Give A Smile team, volunteers, partners, and supporters: It has and continues to be a privilege, honor, and joy to serve alongside you as we change the world one life at a time. I am grateful to each of you for your dedication, your passion to make a difference, your heart to serve, and your love for people. I look forward to all of the great things that are yet to come through our continual work around the world.

To my friends and prayer partners: My heart is full of gratitude toward each of you for your love, support, and encouragement through the various seasons of my life. I am blessed by your continual presence, encouragement, and prayers.

To my Savior, Jesus Christ: Thank You for all You have done for me, for healing and leading me through life, with all of the unexpected turns that have come along the way. Thank You for the dedicated time to complete this project, as I know that Your hand has been on it from start to finish. I am excited for all that lies ahead.

To you: I am grateful to you for taking the time to read this book. My heartfelt prayer is that you have been encouraged to pursue your purpose in life and to continue running the race God has ahead of you!

About the Author

David Rose is an author and speaker who encourages people from all walks of life to press forward to pursue their dreams. His inspiring story has uplifted people of all different backgrounds, setting an example that one's greatest hurts can lead to their biggest ministry. David serves as the President and Founder of To Give A Smile, a nonprofit organization that uplifts and encourages children and their families facing medical-related needs through their outreach efforts, which take place around the world. You can follow David at www.davidallenrose.com.

About To Give A Smile:

To Give A Smile is a non-profit organization geared to reaching children and their families facing medical-related needs. Each year, the organization partners with area children's hospitals and Ronald McDonald Homes to provide fun and uplifting activities to take a child's mind off current treatment. Internationally, the organization takes medical teams all over the world to provide free health-care to children in need. To learn more about To Give A Smile and ways to get involved, visit our website at www.togiveasmile.org.

About Renown Publishing

Renown Publishing was founded with one mission in mind: to make your great idea famous.

At Renown Publishing, we don't just publish. We work hard to pair strategy with innovative marketing techniques so that your book launch is the start of something bigger.

Learn more at RenownPublishing.com.

Notes

1. Gateway Worship. "Alabaster Jar." Track 7 on *Wake Up the World*. Integrity Music, 2008.

2. Johns Hopkins Medicine. "Shunt Procedure." https://www.hopkins medicine.org/neurology_neurosurgery/centers_clinics/cerebral-fluid/procedures/shunts.html.

3. Cleveland Clinic, "tachycardia." Clevelandd Clinic, 2021. https://my.clevelandclinic.org/health/diseases/22108-tachycardia.

4. Crowder, David. "O Praise Him." Track 3 on *Illuminate*. Sixstepsrecords, September 26, 2003.

5. Johns Hopkins Medicine. "Venogram." https://www.hopkins medicine.org/health/treatment-tests-and-therapies/venogram.

6. Johns Hopkins Medicine. "Cerebral Arteriogram." https://www.hopkinsmedicine.org/health/treatment-tests-and-therap ies/cerebral-arteriogram.

7. Mayo Clinic. "Thoracic Outlet Syndrome." https://www.mayo

clinic.org/diseases-conditions/thoracic-outlet-syndrome/symptoms-causes/syc-20353988.

8. Shane & Shane. "When I Think About the Lord." Track 7 on *Carry Away*. Inpop Records, April 22, 2003.

9. Shane & Shane, "When I Think About the Lord."

10. Cleveland Clinic. "Postural Orthostatic Tachycardia Syndrome (POTS)." https://my.clevelandclinic.org/health/diseases/16560-postural-orthostatic-tachycardia-syndrome-pots.

11. Mayo Clinic. "Cardiac Ablation." https://www.mayoclinic.org/tests-procedures/cardiac-ablation/about/pac-20384993.

12. Batterson, Mark. *The Circle Maker: Praying Circles Around Your Biggest Dreams and Greatest Fears*. Zondervan, 2016, p. 27.

13. Reychler, Luc. *Time for Peace: The Essential Role of Time in Conflict and Peace Processes*. University of Queensland Press, 2015.

14. Wallace, Randall. *Secretariat*. Walt Disney Studios Motion Pictures, 2010.

15. History.com. "June 9, 1973: Secretariat Wins Triple Crown in Breathtaking Style." This Day in History. https://www.history.com/this-day-in-history/secretariat-wins-triple-crown.

www.ingramcontent.com/pod-product-compliance
Lightning Source LLC
Chambersburg PA
CBHW070531090426
42735CB00013B/2947